FOCUS GROUP INTERVIEWS IN EDUCATION AND PSYCHOLOGY

FOCUS GROUP INTERVIEWS IN EDUCATION AND PSYCHOLOGY

Sharon Vaughn
Jeanne Shay Schumm
Jane Sinagub

SAGE Publications
International Educational and Professional Publisher
Thousand Oaks   London   New Delhi

For information address:

SAGE Publications, Inc.
2455 Teller Road
Thousand Oaks, California 91320
E-mail: order@sagepub.com

SAGE Publications Ltd.
6 Bonhill Street
London EC2A 4PU
United Kingdom

SAGE Publications India Pvt. Ltd.
M-32 Market
Greater Kailash I
New Delhi 110 048 India

Printed in the United States of America

Library of Congress Cataloging-in-Publication Data

Vaughn, Sharon, 1952-
    Focus group interviews in education and psychology / authors,
  Sharon Vaughn, Jeanne Shay Schumm, Jane M. Sinagub.
        p. cm.
    Includes bibliographical references and index.
    ISBN 0-8039-5892-7 (cloth: acid-free paper.)—
    ISBN 0-8039-5893-5 (pbk.: acid-free paper)
    1. Education—Research—Methodology. 2. Psychology—Research
  Methodology. 3. Focused group interviewing. I. Schumm, Jeanne
  Shay, 1947- . II. Sinagub, Jane M. III. Title.
  LB1028.V38 1996
  370'.78—dc20   95-32521

        97 98 99 10 9 8 7 6 5 4 3 2

This book is printed on acid-free paper.

Sage Production Editor: Diana E. Axelsen
Sage Typesetter: Danielle Dillahunt

CONTENTS

◆ List of Tables   ix

◆ 1 Introduction   xi
       Key Ideas in This Chapter   1
       Background of Focus Group Interviews   2
       Historical Overview of the Focus Group   3
       Definition   4
       Use in Business, Marketing,
           Communication, and Health   7
       Activities   10

◆ 2 Why Use Focus Group Interviews
     in Educational and Psychological
     Research?   12
       Key Ideas in This Chapter   13
       Reason 1: Focus Group Interviews Offer Variety and
           Versatility to Both Qualitative and Quantitative
           Research Methods   14
       Reason 2: Focus Group Interviews Are Compatible
           With the Qualitative Research Paradigm   15
       Reason 3: Focus Group Interviews Offer
           Opportunities for Direct Contact With Subjects   16
       Reason 4: The Group Format Offers Distinctive
           Advantages for Data Collection   18
       The Group Format Promotes Candor
           and Participation   19
       Reason 5: Focus Group Interviews
           Offer Utility   20
       Activities   21

◆ 3 Application of Focus Group
       Interviews for Educational
       and Psychological Research   22
          Key Ideas in This Chapter   23
          Basic Approaches to Research Related to Focus Groups 24
             Exploratory Approach   24
             Clinical Approach   25
             Phenomenological Approach   25
          Applications of Focus Group Interviews   27
             Research Applications   27
          Applications for Policy Development,
             Programming, and Practices   29
             Applications in Action Research   31
             Applications of Focus Groups: A Final Word   33
          Research Questions Appropriate for Focus Group
             Interviews   33
          Activities   35

◆ 4 Preparing for the Focus Group   36
          Key Ideas in This Chapter   37
          Establishing the Purpose   38
          The Moderator's Guide   41
          Number, Time, Size, and Setting of Focus Groups   48
          Activities   55

◆ 5 Selection of Participants   56
          Key Ideas in This Chapter   57
          Developing a Sampling Plan   58
          Establishing Criteria for Sample Selection   60
          Recruiting Participants   64
          Preparing Participants   69
          Activities   73

◆ 6 Role of the Moderator   74
          Key Ideas in This Chapter   75
          The Moderator's Role Within the Focus Group Interview 76
             Planning for the Focus Group   76
             Introductions   77
             Opening the Discussion   78
             Creating and Maintaining a
                Comfortable Environment   79
             Controlling the Topic   81
             Ending the Focus Group Interview   85
          Characteristics of an Effective Moderator   85

Potential Pitfalls for the Moderator 87
Training the Moderator 91
Moderator Aide 93
Activities 94

◆ 7 Data Analysis 96
Key Ideas in This Chapter 97
Qualitative Data Analysis 98
Description of Subjects and Group 99
Considerations Prior to Data Analysis 99
Methods of Analysis 103
Step 1: Identifying the Big Ideas 105
Step 2: Unitizing the Data 105
Step 3: Categorizing the Units 107
Step 4: Negotiating Categories 109
Step 5: Identifying Themes and
Use of Theory 112
Use of Computers for Data Analysis 113
Activities 114

◆ 8 Putting It All Together: Steps in
Conducting Focus Group Interviews 118
Key Ideas in This Chapter 119
Step 1: Delineate the General Purpose 120
Step 2: Designate a Moderator 120
Step 3: Refine the Research Goals 121
Step 4: Select the Participants 121
Step 5: Determine the Number of Focus Group
Interviews 123
Step 6: Arrange for the Focus Group Facility 123
Step 7: Develop an Interview Guide 124
Step 8: Conduct the Focus Group Interview 124
Step 9: Analyze the Focus Group Data 125

◆ 9 Use of Focus Groups With Children
and Adolescents 128
Key Ideas in This Chapter 129
Research Issues in Education and Psychology
That Require Child and Adolescent Subjects 130
Age Limits on Focus Group Participants 132
Group Characteristics 132
Facility Considerations When Working With
Children and Adolescents 133
The Moderator Guide 134
Opening the Focus Group Interview 135

The Role of Parents/Guardians   139
Ethical Considerations   140
Activities   142

◆ **10   Potential Abuses of Focus Group
        Interviews**   **144**
Key Ideas in This Chapter   145
Potential Misuses Before the
    Conduct of the Focus Group   146
    Applicability   146
    Structure   148
    Cost   148
    Role of the Moderator   149
    Participants   150
Potential Misuses During the
    Conduct of the Focus Group   151
    Atmosphere   151
    Participant-Moderator Interaction   152
Potential Misuses After Conduct
    of the Focus Group   153
    Data Analysis and Interpretation   153
    Generalizability of Results   154
Activities   155

◆ **References**   **156**

◆ **Author Index**   **163**

◆ **Subject Index**   **167**

◆ **About the Authors**   **173**

LIST OF TABLES

TABLE 1.1: Procedures for Focus
Groups as Provided in the
Original Descriptive Article   4

TABLE 1.2: Assumptions
Underlying the Focus Group
Interview   7

TABLE 3.1: Sample Research
Questions in Education
Addressed Through Focus
Groups   34

TABLE 3.2: Sample Research
Questions in Psychology
Addressed Through Focus
Groups   34

TABLE 4.1: Overview of the
Sections in the Moderator's
Guide   43

TABLE 4.2: Questions to Address
Prior to Implementing a Focus
Group Interview   49

TABLE 4.3: Location and Facility
Considerations Prior to Focus
Group Interview   53

TABLE 5.1: Pitfalls and
Suggestions for Recruiting
Subjects From School and
Clinical Settings   66

TABLE 5.2: Sample Dialogue for
Recruiting Participants for
Focus Group Interviews   67

TABLE 5.3: Sample Follow-Up
Letter for Recruiting
Participants for Focus
Group Interviews   68

TABLE 5.4: Sample Permission
Form   70

TABLE 5.5: Guidelines for
Encouraging Attendance
and Participant Preparation   73

TABLE 6.1: Contents for the
Moderator's Opening Remarks   80

TABLE 6.2: Excerpts From a
Focus Group Interview   86

TABLE 6.3: Moderator
Characteristics/Skills   88

TABLE 6.4: Questions to Ask
of a Prospective Moderator   89

TABLE 6.5: Moderator Pitfalls   91

TABLE 6.6: Possible
Responsibilities of a
Moderator Aide   93

TABLE 7.1: An Example of
Subject Description Based
on Multiple Focus Group
Interviews   100

TABLE 7.2: Pointers for
Analyzing Focus Group
Interview Data   111

TABLE 7.3 Software Program
Characteristics   115

TABLE 7.4: Names, Addresses,
and Numbers for The
Software Distributors
From TABLE 7.3   116-117

TABLE 8.1: Checklist for
Focus Group Interviews   126

TABLE 9.1: Sample Research
Questions for Child and
Adolescent Participants   130

TABLE 9.2: A Sample Moderator's
Guide for a Focus Group
With Child Participants   136-137

TABLE 9.3: Sample Informed
Consent Form for Children   141

TABLE 10.1: Questions
Inappropriate for Investigations
Using Focus Group Interviews
as the Sole Research Method   147

TABLE 10.2: Potential Budget
Items for Focus Groups   149

INTRODUCTION

OVERVIEW

The purpose of this book is to provide guidelines for the use and application of focus group interviews in education and psychology. Although numerous articles and books address focus groups, most are directed at business and marketing and provide few guidelines and uses for education and psychology. This book is designed to provide sufficient information so that focus group interviews can be used effectively by researchers in education and psychology.

The focus group interview is a research tool that holds great promise for application in educational and psychological research. Other disciplines (e.g., communication, marketing, and advertising) are using focus group interviews to address research issues that cannot be adequately investigated through individual interviews or survey measures alone (Stycos, 1981). This chapter provides the background and history of focus group interviews, a definition of focus group interviews, and the uses of focus groups in disciplines other than education and psychology (e.g., business, marketing).

CHAPTER 1

KEY IDEAS IN THIS CHAPTER

- ◆ Focus groups are increasing in use across disciplines, including education, psychology, marketing, business, health, and communication.

- ◆ Merton developed the focus group interview to determine people's responses to concrete situations and to recurrent experiences.

- ◆ Group discussion distinguishes focus groups from other interview procedures.

- ◆ Although there are a variety of definitions of focus groups, there are several common core elements.

- ◆ Several key uses of the focus group are identified.

Background of
Focus Group Interviews

As Morgan and Krueger (1993) wisely state, "Social science and evaluation research are still at a stage at which most of our knowledge about focus groups comes from personal experience rather than systematic investigation" (p. 3). Despite this dearth of research, the focus group interview is experiencing a boom in use. Although it has been popular as a research technique in the marketing and business areas for more than 30 years, its use has currently expanded to fields such as communication, health, education, and psychology. Nobody knows exactly how many focus groups are conducted each year. An indicator of the popularity of focus groups, however, is that more than 700 rooms throughout the United States have been designated specifically for the use of focus group interviews (Goldman & McDonald, 1987). In fact, focus group interviews have surpassed surveys in the number conducted each year (Goldman & McDonald, 1987). Even presidential advisers have used focus groups to assess reaction to proposed policy (Cannon, 1994).

One possible explanation for the popularity of focus groups is that there is a quick turnaround from implementation to findings. Baker (1985) attributes the boom in the use of focus group interviews to their ability to enable marketing research brand managers (who are under intense pressures to perform) to personally and quickly "experience the consumer experience" (p. 16). There are many, however, who feel that the information provided from focus groups is unique and that their widespread use is therefore a reflection of the expanded knowledge available from focus groups rather than merely a reflection of their efficiency (Baker, 1985).

The impetus for the development of the focus group interview was surveys. Focus group interviews were initially designed to reach beyond the numbers of large sampling polls to discover why people act, think, and feel as they do (Bellenger, Bernhardt, & Goldstucker, 1976; Stycos, 1981). They were also influenced by studies on group dynamics and the effects of the mass media.

Professionals in the fields of marketing and advertising have used focus group interviews extensively because they offer opportunities for businesses to connect to their consumers' perceptions and interests by attempting to ascertain what consumers think about specific products and issues. In education and psychology, focus group interviews offer this same promise. It is becoming increasingly clear that researchers and practitioners in education and psychology (like those in business) need to ascertain the perspectives of key stakeholders, such as clients, parents, teachers, and students.

Historical Overview of the Focus Group

Merton is considered the father of the focus group interview. When he was first hired at Columbia University, Paul Lazarsfeld, already a professor at Columbia, invited Merton to dinner (Merton, 1987). At that time, Lazarsfeld announced that he had wonderful news for Merton. Lazarsfeld had just received a telephone call from the Office of Facts and Figures (the predecessor of the Office of War Information). He informed Merton that the Office of Facts and Figures wanted to know the response of the public to several radio war morale programs, and he invited Merton to join him in conducting the assessments.

When Merton went to the radio studio for the first time, he saw a group of approximately 12 people seated in rows with buttons on the sides of their chairs. They were asked to press a red button when they heard something from a recorded radio program that evoked a negative response and a green button when something they heard evoked a positive response. Merton indicated that this was a new interview situation for him. At the end of the interview process, Lazarsfeld asked Merton what he thought. Merton indicated that he thought the assessment process was interesting and would yield some important findings. He also had some suggestions for an interviewing procedure. That was when Merton initiated the focus group interview.

Merton (1987) indicated that the focus group interview was designed to serve two roles. One was to provide further checks for investigating a concrete experience, such as responses to a film or

TABLE 1.1 Procedures for Focus Groups as Provided in the Original
                Descriptive Article

1. Persons involved in the focus group have witnessed a common event, such as
   heard a radio show or seen a film.

2. The significant elements under investigation have been queried before so that
   the investigator comes to the focus group interview with a set of hypotheses
   concerning their meaning and interpretation.

3. On the basis of previous knowledge, an interview guide is developed.

4. The attention of the focus group interview is on the *subjective experiences* of
   the people exposed to the event. Thus, it was fundamental to the original
   design of the focus group interview that all of the participants had experienced
   a similar, concrete situation.

SOURCE: Adapted from Merton and Kendall (1946).

radio program. The second purpose was to obtain responses to a
recurrent experience, the way focus groups are now frequently used
in the social sciences. Merton acknowledged that the focus group
was no longer the property of market research. Rather, he described
it as "ecumenical." Table 1.1 lists the procedures for focus groups
that were described in Merton's early work.

Definition

Beck, Trombetta, and Share (1986) describe the focus group as
"an informal discussion among selected individuals about specific
topics relevant to the situation at hand" (p. 73). One of the characteristics that distinguishes focus groups from other qualitative interview procedures is the group discussion. The major assumption of
focus groups is that with a permissive atmosphere that fosters a
range of opinions, a more complete and revealing understanding of
the issues will be obtained. Byers and Wilcox (1988) describe focus
groups as discussion groups that address a particular topic or topics.
Krueger (1986) describes focus group interviews as "organized group
discussions which are focused around a single theme" (p. 1). The
goal of focus group interviews is to create a candid, normal conversation that addresses, in depth, the selected topic.

SUMMING UP . . .

Focus group interviews are known by at least three names: focus group interviews, focused interviews, and group depth interviews.

There are a variety of definitions of focus groups. These definitions usually contain the following core elements:

- The group is an informal assembly of target persons whose points of view are requested to address a selected topic.
- The group is small, 6 to 12 members, and is relatively homogeneous.
- A trained moderator with prepared questions and probes sets the stage and induces participants' responses.
- The goal is to elicit perceptions, feelings, attitudes, and ideas of participants about a selected topic.
- Focus groups do not generate quantitative information that can be projected to a larger population.

Folch-Lyon and Trost (1981) indicate that focus group interviews can assist in explaining how and why people behave as they do. Focus groups also provide the means to probe people's emotional reactions to issues. This is particularly relevant in the field of psychology in which further understanding of target individuals' reactions to issues assists in better understanding the research findings. It is important to remember that the purpose of the focus group interview is not on consensus building—rather, it is on obtaining a range of opinions from people about issues.

How do focus groups differ from other small-group interview procedures? In contrast with informal small groups conducted to ascertain people's points of view, focus group interviews are better organized, more formal, and yield findings that result from analysis of the transcriptions from the interviews. A second distinction between focus groups and small groups is that small groups are often used for consensus building or problem solving. It is not an explicit goal in focus groups to reach a consensus. Rather, the goals are to find out each person's point of view and to encourage people to express different points of view. Focus groups are designed to obtain people's opinions and not to determine the exact strength of their opinions. Although the investigator can probe to determine how strongly participants feel, quantitative procedures are more appropriate for ascertaining this information.

Use of Focus Groups. Focus groups are best used when conducting exploratory research. Often the first step in a research study, focus group interviews are followed by subsequent studies designed to refine and further explain the findings. In their original description of the focus group, Merton and Kendall (1946) identified four uses of the focus group interview. First, the focus group interview holds promise for explaining the relationship between a stimulus and an effect. If people are sent brochures about the dangers of smoking and then there is a reduction in that group in smoking, for example, the reasons for the reduction in smoking are not explained. Focus groups can be used to better ascertain and understand the *why* behind such an event by obtaining target people's interpretations of it. Second, the focus group interview can provide information to assist in interpreting unexpected effects, for example, when a subgroup of individuals does not respond as expected. For instance, if findings from a survey revealed that parents of high school students do not want workshops on drug prevention, then focus groups could reveal why. Third, focus group interviews can provide verification in interpreting data that might otherwise only be conjecture. For example, in a survey of factors that inhibit teacher planning for individual student needs, budgetary factors were cited as a primary barrier. It was assumed that budgetary restrictions frequently resulted in increased class size. Focus group interviews could be used to verify this interpretation. Fourth, the focus group interviews can provide alternative interpretations of findings that may not be obtainable using traditional quantitative methods (e.g., why high school students are more likely to complete homework for some teachers than for others). The focus group interview can both unravel fairly complex problems to be pursued through further research procedures and address fairly simple issues. The focus

TABLE 1.2 Assumptions Underlying the Focus Group Interview

1. People are valuable sources of information, particularly about themselves. This assumption, of course, is also inherent within all self-report measures.

2. People are capable of reporting about themselves and are articulate enough to put opinions about their feelings and perceptions into words.

3. The best procedure for obtaining people's feelings and opinions is through a structured group conversation in which information is solicited by the moderator.

4. There are effects of group dynamics that enhance the likelihood that people will speak frankly about a subject, and these cannot occur through individual or small-group interviews. Related to this assumption is that the information obtained from a focus group interview is genuine information about what each person feels rather than a group mind in which people conform to what others believe.

SOURCE: Adapted from Lederman (1990).

group interview can also facilitate decision making and provide further information from the stakeholders. Table 1.2 outlines the assumptions underlying the focus group interview.

Use in Business, Marketing, Communication, and Health

Most of the articles elaborating information on focus groups can be found in marketing and business journals, such as the *Journal of Advertising Research, Marketing News,* and *Marketing Times.* Few articles that describe the use and application of focus groups are available in social science journals. This is particularly interesting because *focus groups are no longer used exclusively in business and marketing.* Focus group interviews are gaining respect in fields such as communication (Byers & Wilcox, 1988) and health (Beck et al., 1986).

Business and Marketing. An article titled "Focus Groups to the Rescue" (Erkut & Fields, 1987) reflects the way in which focus group interviews are currently perceived in much of business and marketing. They are viewed quite positively and as opportunities to reveal how products are perceived policies are evaluated and and the nature of the market for new products. The focus group interview has demonstrated considerable success and utility in the business sector for market research.

When focus group interviews are used in marketing and sales, it is largely to ascertain the public's point of view on a product with the goal in mind to increase sales. These goals are essentially different from those in education and psychology. Often, the goal in marketing research is to determine the extent to which the consumer can be persuaded to purchase a product. Thus, the goal in marketing is often to manipulate or exploit the consumer, whereas in education and psychology, the goal should be to ascertain in the most meaningful way the participants' actual views rather than to persuade the interviewees. Market researchers initiated the use of focus group interviews because they felt there were limitations to traditional sampling pool techniques. They discovered that the focus group interview could provide insights into why persons felt the way they did, not simply the number of individuals who felt a particular way (Calder, 1977; Cox, Higgenbotham, & Burton, 1976).

Communication. The focus group interview was originally used by communication researchers who were interested in the effects of mass media messages. Members of focus groups could be exposed to these media messages and then asked specific questions about their reactions. Focus group interviews have also been used widely to evaluate television and radio shows (Goodman, 1984). This includes using focus groups prior to the release of new shows and to garner information about target groups' reactions to selected topics on shows, reactions to characters, or reactions to roles.

Health. Beck and colleagues (1986) advocate that health practitioners consider the use of focus group interviews before conducting expensive marketing research to determine changes in medical practice. With the move toward community health care, it is not uncommon that physician members of health practices need to determine how community residents will respond to services offered, facilitation locality, and perceptions of the health center. Traditional ways of obtaining this information have been through in-person interviews, mail or telephone interviews, or surveys. Focus groups also provide an effective alternative approach to obtaining health care information (Basch, 1987).

Basch (1987) acknowledges that, although the primary use of focus groups has been in the field of marketing to assess consumers' views about preferences for products, focus groups can also be used in a similar role in health education. Basch advocates the use of focus groups to advance knowledge and provide information dissemination about health education. For example, focus groups can determine core groups' knowledge about nutrition and about how their knowledge influences their practices. Focus groups can also uncover those health-related topics on which core groups would like to have more information. Folch-Lyon and Trost (1981) refer to a study conducted in Mexico that used focus group interviews to better understand the rationales people had for either using or not using contraceptives.

Although focus groups have been touted as risky and perhaps even abused, their use is becoming more prevalent across disciplines (Greenbaum, 1988). In an article about the use of focus group interviews for agricultural educators, Krueger (1986) describes the focus group interview as a "magic box" that facilitates planning and saves time and money. Krueger argues that much of what we do in educational program planning is by trial and error and that much of this trial and error can be eliminated by advanced planning and the application of focus group interviews.

ACTIVITIES

SUMMING UP . . .

Focus group interviews are but one of several research techniques using a group format. Other approaches, which are described in more detail by Stewart and Shamdasani (1990), include the following:

1. Nominal Group Technique: The group often does not meet, but members of the group are individually interviewed and then the findings are summarized.
2. Delphi Technique: This forecast procedure uses experts who are interviewed through a group process.
3. Brainstorming and Synectics: Both of these techniques are designed to encourage creativity and to generate new ideas.
4. Leaderless Discussion Groups: The group is given instructions or a task and then observed to determine the roles that emerge for each of the participants.

ACTIVITIES

1. Read the published speech given by Merton in 1987. How did the name focus group change over time? What is the explanation for this?
2. Identify several topics that you feel would be interesting to pursue as a focus group. Check with your colleagues to get their reactions to the topics you selected.
3. Explain what focus groups are to a friend or family member who is unfamiliar with focus groups. Ask him or her if it would be a good procedure for obtaining information on selected topics.
4. Why do you think focus groups are particularly conducive to use in marketing research? Identify a product that you and several of your friends use frequently. Develop several questions related to the product. In a small, informal group, ask your friends these questions. Evaluate the success of your minifocus group.

WHY USE FOCUS GROUP INTERVIEWS IN EDUCATIONAL AND PSYCHOLOGICAL RESEARCH?

OVERVIEW

Why use focus groups in educational and psychological research? As researchers interested in issues related to education and psychology have begun to espouse a qualitative research paradigm, so also have they explored research tools that can potentially open new vistas to understanding key issues. In this chapter, we will explore the major reasons why many have elected to "borrow" focus group interviews as a research tool from business and marketing: (a) variety and versatility for both qualitative and quantitative research methods, (b) compatibility with the qualitative research paradigm, (c) opportunity for direct contact with subjects, (d) advantages of group format, and (e) utility.

CHAPTER 2

KEY IDEAS IN THIS CHAPTER

- ◆ Focus groups can be used alone or with other methods (qualitative or quantitative) for a wide range of purposes.

- ◆ Focus groups are compatible with the three key assumptions of the qualitative research paradigm.

- ◆ Focus groups offer new dimensions to data collection because of their emphasis on dynamic group interaction.

- ◆ Focus groups can yield a great deal of specific information on a selected topic in a relatively short period of time.

Reason 1: Focus Group Interviews Offer Variety
and Versatility to Both Qualitative
and Quantitative Research Methods.

As a rationale for using focus group interviews in communication research, Byers and Wilcox (1988) offered the following argument:

> It is often said that if you give a small child a hammer, suddenly everything needs to be nailed! So has the "law of the hammer" operated in social science research. One relies on one's well-used or favorite hammers (individual interviews, or survey instruments, or chi squares, or ANOVA, etc.) to generate reliable knowledge. There is always the risk of becoming over zealous with one's favorite research method. The risk is that only certain kinds of inquiries will be raised and answered. Focus groups, as a method of gathering qualitative data, may provide a new opportunity for communication researchers who are tired of the well-used hammers and provide the scientific community with a means of gathering information otherwise not obtainable. (pp. 7-8)

Thus, the focus group interview offers variety to the toolboxes of education and psychology researchers.

DID YOU KNOW THAT?

Perhaps the focus group interview's closest relative is the individual interview. Hess (1968) noted that the focus group interview offers researchers distinct advantages over the individual interview. These include the following:

1. *synergism* (when a wider bank of data emerges through the group interaction),

2. *snowballing* (when the statements of one respondent initiate a chain reaction of additional comments),

3. *stimulation* (when the group discussion generates excitement about a topic),

4. *security* (when the group provides a comfort and encourages candid responses), and

5. *spontaneity* (because participants are not required to answer every question, their responses are more spontaneous and genuine).

Finally, the focus group also offers versatility of use. As described later in this book, focus groups are effective for a wide range of approaches and research purposes. Moreover, focus group interviews can be used alone or with other methods (qualitative or quantitative) to bring an improved depth of understanding to research in education and psychology. Although some investigations have employed focus group interviews as their sole research tool, others have used focus groups as a precursor to an investigation (e.g., the development of a research instrument or design), and some have used focus groups as a follow-up to quantitative investigations (e.g., the verification of findings from survey research). Still others have used focus group interviews simultaneously with other data sources as part of a portfolio of measures to triangulate data (Morgan & Spanish, 1984).

Reason 2: Focus Group Interviews Are Compatible With the Qualitative Research Paradigm.

In both education and psychology, the traditionally maligned qualitative research paradigm has earned greater credence in professional circles within the past decade. Although some trained in the quantitative tradition may be open to the possibilities of qualitative research, some research tools (e.g., life histories, field notes, ethnographies, or participant observation) may seem threatening to researchers who are more accustomed to Likert-type scales. Focus group interviews are planned and structured, but they are also flexible tools that encourage interaction among participants in discussions about target topics.

As Brotherson (1994) explained, focus group interviews are compatible with key assumptions of the qualitative paradigm. First, in the qualitative tradition, the *nature of reality* is viewed as phenomenological, and multiple views of reality can exist. This is a fundamental tenet of focus group interviews. Indeed, one of the strengths of focus group interviews for research in education and psychology is that individuals are invited to participate in a forum where their diverse opinions and perspectives are desired.

Second, adherents of a qualitative paradigm would recognize the potential influence of the *inquirer and respondent relationship*.

In the focus group interview, the interactions between the moderator and respondents and the interactions between the respondents
themselves are recognized as having the potential to add depth and
dimension to the knowledge gained. The moderator is allotted a
great deal of leverage. As Wells (1974) described, "The moderator
works from a list of topics—listening, thinking, probing, exploring,
framing hunches and ideas" (p. 2).

Third, in the qualitative tradition, the *nature of truth statements* is such that truth is influenced by perspective. Truth is
explained by describing a particular set of issues or concepts in
relationship to a particular context. The goal is not to generalize to
larger populations. Rather, the goal is to describe findings within a
particular situation. Thus, with focus group interviews, the intent
is not to elicit principles or tenets that can be extended to a wider
population. The goals are to conduct an interactive discussion that
can elicit a greater, more in-depth understanding of perceptions,
beliefs, attitudes, and experiences from multiple points of view and
to document the context from which those understandings were
derived.

Reason 3: Focus Group Interviews Offer
Opportunities for Direct Contact With Subjects.

Focus group interviews offer researchers in education and psychology the opportunity to garner qualitative data (gathered in
small, interactive groups) regarding the perceptions and opinions of
purposively selected individuals. If conducted properly, the researcher can elicit substantive information about participants'
thoughts and feelings on the topic of interest in relatively little time.
Unlike more impersonal approaches to data collection (e.g., paper
and pencil surveys), focus group interviews have the potential to
bring the investigator closer to the research topic through a direct,
intensive encounter with key individuals. Thus the focus group
interview is a research tool that is highly consistent with current
trends in education and psychology that aim at understanding more
about what key stakeholders think and feel.

For example, Hughes, Schumm, and Vaughn (1994) conducted
an investigation of Hispanic parents' perceptions of reading and

writing activities in the home. The investigation began with a series of focus group interviews to determine what kinds of reading and writing activities were being done and to ascertain the language used to refer to the activities. Transcripts of the interviews were analyzed to identify specific activities that the parents suggested. For example, one frequently mentioned activity was copying from books written in English. Copy work is not an activity classroom teachers typically assign. It is, however, a practice that some parents remembered from their own education and one that they thought would be helpful in teaching their children to write in English. The respondents' comments from the focus group interviews were then used to develop a survey instrument consisting of a list of home literacy activities. Eighty Hispanic parents were then interviewed by telephone to elicit information about the frequency and perceived effectiveness of the various activities.

The overriding assumptions of focus group interviews are that people are valuable sources of information about themselves and that much can be learned from direct, extended conversations with individuals whose thoughts and opinions are critical for understanding a topic (Lederman, 1990). Researchers can gain insights through listening to participants use their words and expressions to communicate their experiences. For example, focus group interviews could be used to examine sources of stress for family members who serve as caretakers for individuals with Alzheimer's disease. Their descriptions of concerns, frustrations, and specific incidents could provide valuable data that are not available from surveys.

Strother (1984) provides evidence that focus group interviews yield more accurate information about what participants actually think than do other research methods. For example, although other formats can reveal that individuals are willing to vote for female political candidates, Strother found that focus group interviews could reveal numerous considerations about that willingness.

Another assumption is that people can describe their perceptions and behaviors (Lederman, 1990). With the guidance of a moderator, individuals are capable of reporting on their own cognitions, feelings, and behaviors in an accurate and forthright manner. Unlike most structured interviews or surveys, participants in focus group interviews have the opportunity to clarify, extend, and provide examples. Moreover, astute moderators can use probes to help participants further direct or amplify their comments. Byers and Wilcox (1988) offered a clear rationale for focus groups: "If we want to know how people felt, what they experienced, what they remembered, what their emotions and motives were like and the reasons for acting as they did—why not just ask them?" (p. 12).

Reason 4: The Group Format Offers
Distinctive Advantages for Data Collection.

Although other research methods (e.g., individual interviews, observations) can bring the researcher in direct, intensive contact with individuals, the interactive group format of focus groups offers distinctive advantages for the collection of rich, in-depth data. First, focus group interviews encourage interaction not only between the moderator and the participants but also between the participants themselves. Second, the group format offers support for individual participants and encourages greater openness in their responses. Third, focus group interviews allow—and even encourage—individuals to form opinions about the designated topic through interaction with others.

The Group Format Is Dynamic. Focus group interviews allow the researcher to witness dynamic, interactive discussion about the designated topics (Morgan & Spanish, 1984). As Brodigan (1992) wrote,

> The feature which most clearly distinguishes focus group research from other kinds of qualitative research is the group discussion. While the discussion centers on issues which are of interest to the researcher, it involves the exchange of opinions, personal reactions, and experience among members of the group. (p. 1)

Similarly, Zeller (1986) observed that the focus group "has the potential of providing a methodology of exploration which allows participants to express their concerns within a context that is useful to the scientific community" (p. 3).

The moderator is guided by a fundamental research question and a well-prepared interview guide. It is likely, however, that the discussion may uncover unanticipated yet relevant issues and concerns. Byers and Wilcox (1991) noted that "it is possible to explore avenues of importance which may arise other than those listed on a questionnaire" (p. 66).

THE GROUP FORMAT PROMOTES CANDOR AND PARTICIPATION

One of the major advantages of focus group interviews is their "loosening effect." In a relaxed group setting where participants sense that their opinions and experiences are valued, participants are more likely to express their opinions and perceptions openly (Byers & Wilcox, 1988). Thus the focus group format facilitates more candid and reflective responses by the participants (Hillebrandt, 1979). Consider the example of a parent of a gifted, elementary school aged student participating in a focus group with other parents of gifted youngsters. The parent commented, "I want my son to have the opportunity to advance more rapidly in math, and, frankly, being in the regular classroom is slowing him down." This remark opened the floodgate, and other parents felt more comfortable about expressing their concerns and experiences.

Fundamental to the focus group interview is the tenet that group interviews can be superior to individual interviews for obtaining perceptions and beliefs (Folch-Lyon & Trost, 1981). The rationale is that the group environment allows greater anonymity and therefore helps individuals to disclose more freely (Beck et al., 1986). In group interviews (unlike individual interviews), a pull for social desirability or a tendency to impress the interviewer may be diminished by the support of peers. Also, the group format itself is active and may stimulate greater participation. Because it is not required that each participant answer every question or respond to every comment (Hisrich & Peters, 1982), the responses that are made may be more genuine and substantial (Schoenfeld, 1988). Moreover, because participants are encouraged to respond openly and freely, focus groups offer the opportunity to elicit a range of opinions (Byers & Wilcox, 1988). Thus, the data available from a focus group interview are often richer and fuller than the data available from an individual interview (Lederman, 1990).

The Group Format Allows Individuals to Form Opinions. There are times when individuals form opinions autonomously and cling to them tenaciously. Other opinions are formed with the direct or indirect input of others and may vacillate or change over periods of time (Krueger, 1988). Although some participants will come to the interview with predetermined opinions, others will be more malleable. The open exchange of different perceptions may spark new opinions or strengthen present convictions (Hillebrandt, 1979; Packard & Dereshiwsky, 1990). For example, such an exchange might be elicited by explaining teachers' perceptions about new school district policies regarding students who speak English as a second language. Indeed, the group interaction approximates the way many individuals come to conclusions and choose actions in consort with others (Calder, 1978; Karger, 1987; Krueger, 1986).

Reason 5: Focus Group Interviews Offer Utility.

A final reason why many researchers in education and psychology are electing to use focus group interviews is that they are less cumbersome than other research methods. Although a great deal of time can and should be spent in preparation of an interview guide and in training the moderator, preparation time is typically far less than the time it takes, for example, to construct a survey instrument or to prepare an observation tool. Focus groups are particularly useful when there is a lack of reliable and valid measures for obtaining information on the selected topics. For example, focus group interviews could be appropriate for examining Hispanic adolescents' relationships with stepparents when no survey instrument or observation measure is available. Moreover, focus group interviews have a quick turnaround time in data collection. Thus, in a relatively short period of time (i.e., typical focus groups last approximately 90 minutes), researchers can gather specific information on selected topics.

Similarly, when used for program development or evaluation, the findings of focus group interviews can be used to initiate programmatic change. For example, focus group interviews of tutors working with at-risk elementary school students can be conducted to evaluate tutor training procedures as well as practices used to support tutors in the field.

ACTIVITIES

1. This chapter presents five major reasons for using focus group interviews. Each reason could be interpreted as an "advantage." For each of the "advantages," develop a counterargument or a related "disadvantage." Discuss your list of disadvantages with your colleagues.

2. Identify a research question for which a *survey* would be a more appropriate research tool than a focus group interview. Identify a research question for which an *individual interview* would be a more appropriate research tool than a focus group interview.

3. Focus group interviews operate under the assumption that people can articulate their perceptions and behaviors. Describe a hypothetical focus group situation that would inhibit or discourage individuals from active, open participation.

4. Focus group interviews are described by some authors as well-planned and structured, yet flexible and relaxed. Discuss with a group of your colleagues how a balance between structure and flexibility might be achieved.

ACTIVITIES

APPLICATION OF FOCUS GROUP INTERVIEWS FOR EDUCATIONAL AND PSYCHOLOGICAL RESEARCH

OVERVIEW

One of the most inviting aspects of focus group interviews is their versatility. This chapter provides a window on this versatility by presenting an array of applications of focus group interviews for education and psychology. It begins with an explanation of the basic research approaches most compatible with focus groups. It continues with suggested applications for research and program planning and evaluation. The chapter concludes with examples of research questions in education and psychology that can be addressed through focus group interviews.

CHAPTER 3

KEY IDEAS IN THIS CHAPTER

◆ Focus group interviews are appropriate for a number of research approaches: exploratory, clinical, and phenomenological.

◆ For research studies, focus group interviews can be used in development of hypotheses and instruments, refinement of research designs, and interpretation of consistent findings.

◆ Focus group interviews can be used for program planning and evaluation.

◆ Focus group interviews can be used as the sole research tool or in conjunction with other research methods.

◆ Research questions most appropriate for focus group interviews are those related to exploratory or explanatory issues.

◆ Research questions most inappropriate for focus group interviews are those designed to determine prevalence or that are predictive in nature.

Basic Approaches to
Research Related to Focus Groups

Calder (1977) defined three basic approaches to research that apply to focus group interviews: exploratory, clinical (judgment), and phenomenological. Each is appropriate for collecting specific types of information. In building a rationale for using focus group interviews, the researcher must consider whether the purpose for conducting the study is consistent with one or more of these approaches.

EXPLORATORY APPROACH

The purpose of the exploratory approach to research is to investigate areas that are relatively unknown and to obtain "prescientific knowledge" (Calder, 1977, p. 355). The approach is viewed as prescientific because its goal is to generate ideas and to validate these ideas against the everyday experiences of target subjects. Focus groups are particularly useful for exploratory research when little is known about the topic (Brodigan, 1992; Hisrich & Peters, 1982). This is particularly important in education and psychology because this approach can be used to collect descriptive information or pilot knowledge to explicate and better understand constructs and to generate hypotheses. It can also be used to test (against the everyday experiences of selected target individuals) initial ideas for hypotheses, research issues, and research designs (e.g., Baca, 1989).

Thus, exploratory focus groups are often a first step preceding more ambitious efforts. The work of Mays, Cochran, and Bellinger (1992) provides an example. These researchers used focus group interviews to develop an awareness of the sexual vocabulary of African American gay men. The authors were interested in learning about the terminology used by this group to develop appropriate AIDS prevention interventions. At the beginning of each focus group, participants were given a list of terms referring to sexual behaviors. The moderator read each term aloud and the participants were asked about their familiarity with the terms and how the terms were used in their vernacular. Participants also were asked to list any other terms that would be a part of their sexual language. The list of terms from the focus group interviews were then used to develop a sexual behavior inventory. This inventory was distributed to gay African American and white subjects to determine their level of familiarity with the terms and to determine which terms were unique to the African American gay community.

CLINICAL APPROACH

The clinical or therapeutic approach is influenced by clinical psychology in that its purpose is to provide a "psychological loosening effect" of the group to get beyond superficial self-reports and to delve into emotions and unconscious motives related to the topic (Durgee, 1986, p. 58). Calder (1977) labeled this approach as quasi-scientific in that the researchers' knowledge of the constructs and theories pertaining to the topic are used to guide in-depth probing and careful observation of verbal and nonverbal responses during the interview and analysis and interpretation of the data following the interview. Thus this approach is highly dependent on the level of knowledge of the individuals who conduct and interpret data and on the degree to which that knowledge is based on scientific theories and constructs rather than simple intuition or personal experience.

For example, focus group interviews could be conducted to ascertain elementary school teachers' beliefs about how reading acquisition occurs. In the clinical approach, the moderator would be highly familiar with theoretical models of the reading acquisition. The moderator would structure probes that would uncover reasons for espousing particular beliefs and would encourage a high degree of group interaction to trigger emotional, unguarded reactions.

PHENOMENOLOGICAL APPROACH

Perhaps the most common approach to focus group interviews is the phenomenological approach. The purpose of this approach is to understand the issue or topic from the everyday knowledge and perceptions of specific respondent subgroups (Lindgren & Kehoe, 1981). In this approach (unlike the exploratory approach), researchers have initial knowledge about the topic and are interested in developing a more in-depth understanding or in clarifying potentially conflicting or equivocal information from previous data. As Calder (1977) wrote,

> The logic of the phenomenological approach dictates that the researcher have close personal involvement with consumers. He or she must share, participatively or vicariously, the experience of consumers. It is misleading, on reflection, to say that the value of phenomenological focus groups is in the experiencing of consumers. What they should yield is the experiencing of the experience of consumers. (p. 360)

An example of a study implementing a phenomenological approach is one conducted by Schumm, Vaughn, Elbaum, and Moody (1995). This research team conducted a yearlong study of teachers' perceptions of grouping practices for reading instruction. Participating teachers completed survey instruments, participated in individual interviews, and were observed three times during the school year. Analyses of these data revealed initial trends and issues. A series of focus group interviews were then conducted to confirm findings and to clarify ambiguities. For example, one trend was the prevailing use of whole-class instruction followed by independent practice. During the focus group interviews, teachers explained why they found this practice to be particularly feasible in respect to classroom management: They no longer felt fragmented by dividing their time among small instructional groups. They also explained that this formation was a practical necessity because some schools elected to issue only one level of the basal reader to each class. Thus the focus groups enabled the research team to explore themes in greater depth and to clear up discrepancies.

SUMMING UP . . .

Bauman and Adair (1992) suggested that the focus group interview is helpful in the collection of four types of data: (a) *range*, a full spectrum of responses to a stimulus or issue; (b) *specificity*, detail about reactions and responses; (c) *depth*, a rich understanding of cognitive and affective responses; and (d) *personal context*, information regarding characteristics and experiences influencing responses.

Applications of Focus Group Interviews

RESEARCH APPLICATIONS

Hypothesis Development. Hypothesis formulation is typically based on the researchers' interpretations of related theoretical and empirical evidence. The most conservative use of the focus group interview is for developing hypotheses for further quantitative or qualitative exploration (Basch, 1987; Calder, 1978; Hisrich & Peters, 1982; Morgan & Spanish, 1984; Rosenstein, 1976; Stycos, 1981). For example, a researcher interested in parents' perceptions of the prereferral process for students who are potentially eligible for gifted education programs could conduct focus group interviews. These interviews could produce data helpful in generating hypotheses for further evaluation through both qualitative and quantitative methodologies.

Furthermore, focus groups can be used as an initial test of hypotheses before conducting a larger study. After hypotheses are generated, it is often useful to obtain the perceptions and feedback of selected individuals to further refine the hypotheses and research design (Goodman, 1984). For example, it may be hypothesized that individuals enrolled in a smoking cessation program involving one-to-one peer counseling would differ in their success rates for breaking the habit from those involved in group counseling sessions. Focus group interviews with individuals involved in both program types could be conducted to further clarify the hypothesis.

Instrument Development. Focus group interviews can be helpful in the development of questionnaires, surveys, and items for tests ("A Step-By-Step," 1978; Goodman, 1984; Hisrich & Peters, 1982; Mates & Allison, 1992). Focus group findings can assist in identifying response categories and constructs that researchers might not have otherwise considered. In using focus groups, the items that are most relevant from the subjects' perspective are less likely to be overlooked (Basch, 1987).

For example, Yuhas (1986) could not find an appropriate measure for her topic of interest—romantic jealousy in marriage. She conducted a series of four focus group interviews to identify major issues, and they enabled her to better understand the confusion individuals have about certain constructs (e.g., the distinction between marital jealousy, envy, and anger). Yuhas also uncovered issues that had not previously been identified (e.g., the relationship between jealousy and masculinity).

Focus groups can make research instruments more language sensitive because vocabulary that is common to the stakeholders can be discerned in the focus groups and then incorporated into the measure (Bauman & Adair, 1992; Hammond, 1986). In the romantic jealousy example above, Yuhas (1986) was able to glean the language couples typically use to communicate about this topic and then to incorporate that language in a subsequent scale.

If the goal is to develop forced-choice responses, focus groups can assist in developing and refining the alternative responses that are feasible. Participants can be asked to complete a survey and then, during a focus group, to critique the alternative responses. In addition, after an instrument prototype has been drafted, focus groups can be used as part of the field testing of the measure. A group of subjects can complete the instrument and then evaluate the administration procedures, form, and content.

Fine-Tuning Research Designs. Research in education and psychology—particularly applied research—must operate in the context of the "real world." The success of any research project is frequently dependent on the ability of the researcher to anticipate potential quandaries in research designs and procedures that relate to the context in which the research is conducted. Focus group interviews can help in fine-tuning qualitative or quantitative research designs and in aiding the researcher to forecast and plan for potentially troublesome factors. An example is an intervention study designed to have elementary students serve as teachers in a scaffolded-learning approach to content reading instruction. Focus group interviews with 3rd- and 4th-grade teachers (the target grades for the study) were conducted to determine their perceptions of the feasibility of the designated procedures (Vaughn, Klingner, & Schumm, 1994).

Interpretation of Findings. Focus group interviews are a tool for obtaining the perceptions and interpretations of key stakeholders regarding research findings. The use of focus groups is what people in marketing research refer to as "returning to the well." In education and psychology, the way this can be applied is by returning to key stakeholders who are actually working with, or are invested in, the topic of our research and asking them to provide their interpretation of the findings or suggestions for further research. Consider the example of a survey of teachers on the effects of grouping practices during reading instruction on the academic and social progress of elementary school students. If the findings of this study were presented to a focus group of teachers, data about their perceptions of the findings and the type of questions they feel are important to address in the future could be obtained.

It may well be that, after a series of focus group interviews is conducted and data analyzed, additional interviews will be necessary to clarify or amplify data. In an article by Bertrand, Ward, and Pauc (1992), focus group research was used to learn about the sexual behavior and practices of the Mayan population and their resistance to family planning. Nine focus group interviews were conducted using the initial set of questions. After data analysis, the researchers realized that additional information was needed on particular questions, and four additional focus group interviews were conducted.

Focus group interviews can also be used to determine the perceptions of individuals who participate in a research study. For example, teachers involved in yearlong case studies of general education teachers' planning for students with disabilities were interviewed to determine what aspects of the study they found beneficial, what their perceptions of the study were, and what suggestions for changes they would make if the study were conducted again (Schumm, Vaughn, Haager, et al., 1995). Findings from these focus groups can be used by the investigators in designing and implementing future studies.

Applications for Policy Development, Programming, and Practices

Focus groups provide an opportunity to obtain the perceptions and attitudes of key stakeholders regarding new policies or movements. Focus groups can also assist in determining key stakeholders' reactions to proposed or existing programs, practices, curricula, instructional methods, schedules, and so on (e.g., Elliott, 1989; Miller, 1987). Obviously, these applications can occur before, during, or after the implementation of the policy, program, or practice. Focus groups are particularly helpful for planning, for needs assessments, and for program evaluation.

Planning for Policies, Programs, and Practices. Whether policies are developed on a local, state, or national level, focus group interviews can be used to determine the positions of key stakeholders. Similarly, before the initiation of new programs or practices, focus groups can be used to determine stakeholder interest, enthusiasm, and perceptions of potential pitfalls. Examples of applications of focus group interviews for planning purposes are profuse:

- The Minnesota Extension Service (Krueger, 1986) used focus groups to identify course offerings of interest to target populations.
- At Beloit College (Brodigan, 1992), focus group interviews are a process of acquiring more information about prospective students.
- According to Buttram (1991), focus group interviews are used by the Research for Better Schools Incorporated of Philadelphia on a yearly basis as part of a research for better schools planning process. They consider the focus group interview as an opportunity to "eavesdrop" as educators discuss the critical issues with respect to school restructuring.
- At community colleges, focus group interviews have been used to determine ways of better serving diverse student populations, including students who are high risk and delayed entry students (Cohen & Engleberg, 1989).
- Gold and Kelly (1991) used focus group interviews as a means to obtain information on related AIDS educational programs and materials. The questions of interest included the cultural sensitivity of the AIDS material, the best format for AIDS materials, and the key characteristics and concepts important for effective AIDS education.

Needs Assessments. Focus groups can also be used to clarify needs and to develop needs assessment surveys (e.g., Antonucci, 1989; Buttram, 1990, 1991; McCormick, 1987). Buttram (1990) wrote,

> Since most formal needs assessments involve large numbers of individuals, more open-ended assessments that do not supply predetermined lists of needs are seldom feasible. Yet it is in these very incidences that needs assessments are so crucial to ensure that the program will be responsive to the target group. Focus groups . . . can help resolve a dilemma involved in developing that initial list. (p. 3)

For example, in the area of professional development, we conducted focus groups with teachers for whom a course was planned (Schumm, Vaughn, & Leavell, 1994). Based on the topics generated from the focus groups, a needs assessment instrument was developed, which was used to have course participants prioritize topics of interest.

Another possible application would be for faculty members at a university to participate in a focus group interview to determine their professional development needs related to classroom instruction. The information could be used to develop workshops sponsored by a center for professional improvement.

Consumer Satisfaction and Evaluation. Focus groups can be used to measure consumer satisfaction after a policy, program, or practice has been implemented (e.g., Black, 1989; Connors, 1991; Hanson, 1991; Redfield & Craig, 1988). For example, parents' reactions to the implementation of a policy for wearing school uniforms in a public school can be gauged using focus groups. Similarly, students' perceptions of a potential change in course requirements could be obtained to determine consumer satisfaction and recommendations for program improvement.

Also, members of the legal profession have started to use focus group interviews as part of pretrial preparation. The format has been helpful for testing courtroom strategies and tactics and for predicting juror responses.

APPLICATIONS IN ACTION RESEARCH

Traditionally, empirical investigation has been primarily in the hands of formally trained researchers. In recent years, a movement has been underway to bridge the gap between researchers and practitioners and to encourage site-based research that directly impacts practice. Practitioners have been encouraged to become actively involved in what is called *action research*. This trend has been particularly strong in education in what is known as *the teacher-as-researcher movement* (Patterson, Santa, Short, & Smith, 1993). In this movement, partnerships of teachers, teachers and administrators, and teachers and university researchers have been formed to explore research topics that are of interest to teachers and that have direct bearing on classroom practice. Possible uses for focus groups in action research include needs assessments for parenting workshops and student reactions to new instructional practices.

Because focus group interviews have the potential to elicit a great deal of information in a short period of time from those most directly involved, this method has promise in action research. Focus group interviews, however, are not for the novice or inexperienced researcher, and (as Chapter 10 will detail) there are many potential abuses of focus group interviews that can impact the validity of results as well as the relationships with participants and target audiences.

SUMMING UP . . .

In a discussion of erroneous assumptions about focus groups, Bers (1989) addressed the common misconception that "focus group research is soft and fuzzy, and anybody can do it" (p. 261). Bers argued that "focus-group research is based upon well-developed principles of psychology, sociology, and communication. Researchers using the methodology must be familiar with the application of these principles even if they are not conversant with the theories or empirical studies comprising them" (p. 262).

In considering the use of focus group interviews with action research, several cautions and comments seem appropriate. Ostensibly, the potential user of focus groups should be aware of the possibilities and limitations of focus groups as well as the steps for their proper conduct and interpretation. Complex data analysis techniques may not be appropriate for practitioners, but more informal data analysis can be implemented to inform practice. For example, audio scanning of interview tapes may be more feasible than transcription. Most significantly, ethical issues (e.g., how student comments during a focus group might impact their grades or how parents' reactions to schoolwide programs might influence one teacher's professional standing) should be considered. Action researchers should carefully plan and anticipate how findings will be used and the impact of dissemination of findings on key stakeholders.

APPLICATIONS OF FOCUS GROUPS: A FINAL WORD

A common misconception is that focus group interviews are used primarily for gauging consumer reaction to a product or marketing technique. On the contrary, focus group interviews are a versatile tool that can be used alone or with other methods (qualitative or quantitative) to bring an improved depth of understanding to research in education and psychology.

Although not specifically stated, it should be apparent by now that focus groups can be used in conjunction with other research methods in exploratory or confirmatory functions. A focus group interview or, preferably, a series of focus group interviews can also be used as the sole research tool for a study. For example, a series of focus group interviews was conducted with subgroups of teachers (e.g., special education, reading specialists, general education teachers) to learn about their perceptions regarding the inclusion of students with disabilities in the general education classroom (Vaughn, Schumm, Jallad, Slusher, & Saumell, in press).

Research Questions Appropriate for Focus Group Interviews

Another decision that must be addressed when considering the use of focus group interviews is whether this research tool fits the

Sample Research Questions in Education Addressed
Through Focus Groups

1. What are teachers' perceptions of the effects of portfolio assessment on student learning, especially for at-risk students (Wolf, 1991)?

2. What are mainland Puerto Rican students' concerns related to ethnic identity (Marsiglia & Halasa, 1992)?

3. What are general education teachers' perceptions of the desirability and feasibility of adaptations for mainstreamed special education students (Schumm & Vaughn, 1991)?

4. What are the sources of math anxiety among college students (Dellens, 1979)?

5. What are community leaders' (e.g., church leaders, police and fire chiefs, business and political leaders) perceptions of early childhood education (Connors, 1991)?

research questions. In other words, can the focus group interview facilitate finding answers to the intended questions? The reality is that focus group interviews are more appropriate for some research questions than others. Focus group interviews are most appropriate for questions related to research that is exploratory or explanatory in nature. Sample research questions in education that can be addressed through focus groups are provided in Table 3.1; research questions in psychology are provided in Table 3.2.

TABLE 3.2 Sample Research Questions in Psychology Addressed
Through Focus Groups

1. What are the differences between mothers and fathers as sexuality educators and between daughters and sons as recipients of parental communication about sexuality (Nolan & Petersen, 1992)?

2. What are the coping responses of older parents whose adult children are undergoing a divorce (Hamon & Thiessen, 1990)?

3. What are the attitudes of family caregivers toward community psychological support services (Collins, Stommel, King, & Given, 1991)?

4. What are adult asthma patients' perceptions of changes in their quality of life (Hyland, Finnis, & Irvine, 1990)?

5. What are the perceptions of parents in city centers regarding how to recruit difficult-to-reach families (i.e., families with alcohol problems) in an intervention aimed at preventing mental health problems and alcoholism in children (Lengua, et al., 1992)?

ACTIVITIES

1. Construct research questions that would be appropriate for studies employing focus group interviews in each of the three basic approaches: exploratory, clinical, and phenomenological.

2. You are planning an investigation exploring the impact of neighborhood violence on children's sense of security and well-being. You are particularly interested in the perceptions of Hispanic parents from a large urban community. How might focus group interviews be used effectively in your investigation?

3. You are planning a program to educate youths in a rural area about safe sex. How might you use focus group interviews in the planning and evaluation of this program?

4. You are preparing a research grant proposal to submit to a federal agency. How might you use focus group interviews to develop and enhance your proposal?

ACTIVITIES

PREPARING FOR THE FOCUS GROUP

OVERVIEW

Focus group interviews appear deceptively easy to implement, and, therefore, they are frequently misused. Perhaps the mistake most commonly made is lack of adequate preparation for the implementation of focus groups. This chapter will address the essential steps in preparing adequately for the conduct of the focus group. These steps include (a) establishing the purpose of the focus group, including its goals and desired outcomes; (b) developing the moderator's guide; (c) determining the number of focus groups that will likely be needed; and (d) selecting the location.

CHAPTER 4

KEY IDEAS IN THIS CHAPTER

◆ The general purpose statement should be agreed on by all members of the research team and should provide an orientation to the focus group.

◆ A more refined purpose statement includes a list of the information one does and does not want to know from the focus group.

◆ Two sets of goals are written prior to implementing the focus group: (a) how information will be used and (b) the outcomes desired.

◆ The moderator's guide contains several key elements: (a) introduction, (b) warm-up, (c) clarification of terms, (d) easy and nonthreatening questions, (e) more difficult questions, (f) wrap-up, (g) member check, and (h) closing statements.

◆ The purpose and goals provide the guidelines for the number of focus groups conducted.

◆ The number of focus groups is determined by convergence of findings and the extent to which all subgroups are represented.

◆ Eight to ten participants is the ideal size for a focus group.

◆ The setting is an integral component to the success of the focus group, and several considerations should be followed.

Establishing the Purpose

Research using focus groups does not differ from other research in that the success of the project is directly related to how clearly the research problem is identified. Establishing the purpose of the focus group is essential to its success because the purpose lays the ground work for subsequent decisions. Thus, the purpose and goals assist the researcher in determining the sampling plan, the number of focus groups needed, the questions and probes, and a means for evaluating whether adequate information has been obtained or whether subsequent focus groups need to be conducted.

General Purpose Statement. The first step is to establish a general purpose statement that reflects an overall summary of the researchers' interests. This general statement should be read and agreed on by all interested members of the research team. The general purpose statement may be as brief as one sentence or as long as several paragraphs. It is essential that the researcher clearly identify the topic to be discussed and limit the range of topics and ideas. It is better to limit the scope of the focus group to a specific topic than it is to attempt to accomplish too much.

A psychologist was interested in using focus group interviews to determine individuals' reactions to Hurricane Andrew. She felt the information would be helpful to her as she developed a measure assessing individuals' levels of anxiety immediately following and then several months after Hurricane Andrew struck southern Florida. She wrote the following general purpose statement:

> The purpose of these focus group interviews is to ascertain adults' emotional reactions to Hurricane Andrew. I am particularly interested in the extent to which they felt anxious immediately following the hurricane and how these reactions compare with how they feel now.

Her next step was to further refine and define her general statement.

Refining the Purpose Statement. A general purpose statement provides an orientation to the intent of the focus group, but it is an inadequate source for the development of questions and probes.

Furthermore, it is essential that the purpose be delineated. Otherwise, the moderator will be unsure when to probe and whether the focus group has adequately addressed the purpose. One of the first steps in refining the purpose statement is the development of a list of information that the researcher *does* and *does not* want to obtain from the focus group. My colleague interested in using focus groups for determining anxiety levels after Hurricane Andrew prepared the following lists:

Do Want to Know:

1. How adults felt *in general* during the hurricane. Encourage the use of *emotion* words and phrases.
2. The extent to which they were fearful or anxious during the hurricane.
3. The extent to which they still have *feelings* related to the hurricane.
4. The extent to which they are still fearful or anxious.
5. Ways they perceive the hurricane affected them emotionally.

Do Not Want to Know:

1. How they feel in general now.
2. What damage they incurred and what pieces of property were affected.
3. How they think others feel (e.g., their neighbors, friends, or other relatives).
4. How they feel about living in south Florida now that the hurricane has struck.

Identifying Goals. After the purpose statement has been refined and the information of interest has been clarified, the research goals need to be specified. The first part of establishing the research goals is to identify what specific question or aspect of the research study the focus group is designed to address. Focus groups can be used as the sole methodology or as the first step in a research study. The information garnered from the focus group is used to inform other aspects of the study.

There are two types of goals that need to be established for focus groups. The first set of goals relates to how the information gleaned from the focus groups will be used. The second set of goals is written to identify the outcomes required for the focus group to be successful.

To achieve the first goal, uses of the focus group need to be identified. Some examples of the common uses of focus groups are the following:

- Develop a general understanding of target groups' perceptions of a specified topic.

- Identify the language and key concepts that target groups use to discuss a specific topic or issue.

- Generate research hypotheses that can be further developed and tested using other research approaches.

- Field test a research procedure, measure, or reaction to a set of research procedures that the researcher intends to implement.

- Solicit ideas that relate to the topic of interest to determine whether the identified research questions are complete and represent those that are viewed as important by key stakeholders.

- Interpret or validate quantitative data that have been previously obtained.

- Extend findings from qualitative data obtained from other sources.

To achieve the second goal, specific outcomes that relate to the focus group need to be identified. These outcomes often include one or more of the following:

- Key ideas that relate to the topic are identified.

- The importance or significance of these key ideas can be described.

- How strongly the participants feel about these key ideas can be identified.

- Language and vocabulary are identified that relate to the issue and can be used in the design of measures and in communication with participants.

- Questions and information from participants are available to assist with the further development of the research questions and purposes.

- Information from participants verifies hypotheses or helps in refining hypotheses.

After the purpose and goals for the focus group are es
the researcher is prepared to make decisions regarding t
of the research questions, probes, and the developme
moderator's guide.

The Moderator's Guide

After carefully considering the research questions and the information that the researcher does and does not want to obtain, it
is necessary to develop a moderator's guide. The purpose of the
moderator's guide is to serve as a *map* to chart the course of the
focus group interview from beginning to end. As is true for persons
planning a trip, the range of details provided in the moderator's
guide varies considerably: It can be excessively detailed (e.g., including all probes and responses), or it can be a general plan providing
the major questions and probes but little else. The level of detail
required for the moderator's plan is directly related to the moderator's experience and comfort level with the conduct of focus groups
and the topic discussed.

The following sections are needed in the moderator's guide: (a)
introduction, (b) warm-up, (c) clarification of terms, (d) easy and
nonthreatening questions, (e) more difficult questions, (f) wrap-up,
(g) member check, and (h) closing statements. Each of these sections
will be discussed and examples provided. An overview of each of the
sections in the moderator's guide is provided in Table 4.1.

Introduction. The purpose of the introduction is to provide an
overview of the topic of the focus group interview, to establish the
guidelines for how the interview will proceed, and to set the tone
for how the interview will be conducted. The following is a sample
introduction.

Welcome. *"Welcome and thank you for coming to this focus group.
Each of you has been selected to participate because your point
of view is important to us. We know that you are very busy and
we greatly appreciate your contribution to this project. This
interview is not a test, nor should it in any way be viewed as a*

series of questions with right or wrong answers. Remember, we are very interested in what you think and feel. We want to know your opinions on these issues, and we are certainly not interested in your agreeing with the opinions and feelings of others. There may be times, however, when you do, and it is appropriate for you to let us know that as well."

Purpose. *"The purpose of this focus group interview is to determine your ideas and opinions about the topic of inclusion of students with mild-to-moderate disabilities in general education classrooms."*

Guidelines. *"There are a few guidelines I would like to ask you to follow during the focus group interview. First, you do not need to speak in any particular order. When you have something to say, please do so. Second, please do not speak while someone else is talking. Sometimes, the exchanges get emotional, and it is tempting to 'jump in' when someone is talking, but we ask you to refrain from doing so. Third, remember that there are many people in the group and that it is important that we obtain the point of view of each one of you. Fourth, you do not need to agree with what everyone or anyone in the group says, but you do need to state your point of view without making any negative comments or 'put downs.' Finally, because we have limited time together, I may need to stop you and to redirect our discussion. What questions do you have? . . . Okay, let's begin."*

Warm-Up. The warm-up provides an opportunity for the moderator to ask general introductory questions to set the focus group participants at ease and to prepare them for the more challenging questions. Allow each participant 2 to 3 minutes to address these warm-up questions. The following is an example of a warm-up.

Warm-Up. *"During the reception, you had an opportunity to meet each other and to ask each other questions. You probably discovered that each one of you is presently working as a teacher in a local school, although no two of you are from the same school. Briefly, tell each of us how long you have been teaching*

TABLE 4.1 Overview of the Sections in the Moderator's Guide

   I. Introduction
      A. Welcome
      B. Statement of the purpose of the interview
      C. Guidelines to follow during the interview
  II. Warm-Up
      A. Set the tone
      B. Set participants at ease
 III. Clarification of Terms
      A. Establish the knowledge base of key terms through questions
      B. Provide definitions of key terms
  IV. Establish Easy and Nonthreatening Questions
      A. The initial questions should be general and less threatening
   V. Establish More Difficult Questions
      A. The more difficult or personal questions should be determined
  VI. Wrap-Up
      A. Identify and organize the major themes from the participant's responses
      B. Ensure that any conversational points not completed are mentioned
 VII. Member Check
      A. Determine how each member perceives selected issues
VIII. Closing Statements
      A. Request anonymity of information
      B. Answer any remaining questions
      C. Express thanks

---

and whether you have had students with mild-to-moderate disabilities in your classroom."

Clarification of Terms. Before the more challenging questions are asked, it is important to clarify any terms that may be used in the questions or that are likely to occur in the conversation. This provides a common knowledge base for all of the participants. Terms are sometimes clarified by the moderator asking questions about the terms and then connecting and expanding on respondents' answers. Terms are also clarified by the moderator defining them for the participants. In the following examples, questions are used for the terms *mainstreaming* and *inclusion.* The moderator decided to provide a definition of mild-to-moderate disabilities for two reasons: (a) to save time and (b) because participants were likely to define this term in different ways.

"Many of you in education are familiar with the term mainstreaming. In your own words, what would you say mainstreaming means?"

Allow several participants to respond, and then use their responses to connect the aspects of their responses that were correct and to provide clarification on the correct response.

"Inclusion is a relatively new term, and yet it has appeared in articles in newspapers, magazines, and professional journals. What do you know about inclusion?"

Be sure to clarify the ways in which mainstreaming and inclusion are the same and different.

"For the purpose of this interview, the term mild-to-moderate disabilities refers to mild cognitive and behavior problems that interfere with students' learning—problems such as learning disabilities, mild mental retardation, mild attention problems, and mild behavior problems."

Easy and Nonthreatening Questions. The initial questions are more general and are nonthreatening. These questions allow the group time to understand the interview process and to feel more comfortable expressing their points of view.

"What are some of the reasons why teachers or parents might want to include students with mild-to-moderate disabilities in general education classrooms?"

"What are some of the reasons why teachers or parents might not want to include students with mild-to-moderate disabilities in general education classrooms?"

Probe for reasons that reflect the perspectives of both teachers and parents.)

"How do you think decisions are made about the placement of students with mild-to-moderate disabilities in general education classrooms?"

Follow-up question: *"To what extent do you think teachers will be involved in that decision?"*

More Difficult Questions. As participants feel more comfortable with the interview process, the moderator asks more difficult questions. Often this means questions that require participants to state their opinion or to provide rationales for their feelings.

"How would you feel if students with mild-to-moderate disabilities were placed in your classroom for the entire day?

What kind of support would you need if students with mild-to-moderate disabilities were placed in your classroom for the entire day?

What would be some of the barriers and facilitators to the success of students with mild-to-moderate disabilities who were placed in general education classrooms all day?

To what extent do you feel that, as a teacher, you are prepared to meet the educational and social needs of students with mild-to-moderate disabilities placed in your classroom?

Overall, what is your opinion about what would happen if inclusion of students with disabilities were part of your school's program?"

Wrap-Up. During the wrap-up, the moderator's goal is twofold. First, the moderator attempts to identify the major *themes* of the participants' responses and to organize these in a summative manner. Second, the moderator aims to ensure that any conversational points that were not completed are recognized. The following is an example of the first part of a wrap-up or the *summary*.

"Unfortunately, we are close to being out of time. As I mentioned to you on the telephone, once the interview gets started it moves

at a fast pace, and there is less time to express your points of view than we would like. Let me attempt to summarize the key ideas I have heard. One key idea is that administrators are unaware of the demands placed on teachers and often make decisions with little understanding of the reality of implementing those decisions. Second, because parents want what is best for their children, they are often unaware of the difficulty of meeting the individual needs of 34 students. Third, teachers are concerned about the welfare of all children and are willing to make accommodations that are realistic and feasible for students with mild-to-moderate disabilities. But they cannot be expected to replace special services needed by the students. Fourth, many teachers do not feel that they have the skills and confidence to meet the educational and social needs of students in their classrooms with mild-to-moderate disabilities. Finally, teachers fear many negative consequences of inclusion—for example, reduced assistance from specialized personnel, such as the special education teacher; lack of adequate resources, such as books and computers; and lawsuits from parents. What would you like to add to my summary?"

The second part of the wrap-up is for the moderator to ensure that any conversational points that were not completed are recognized. It is important that the moderator indicate that not all questions can be discussed as fully as all group members would like.

"There were several topics that we touched upon and that we were not able to complete discussing during this focus group. Several of you expressed concerns about mandates from the federal or state level that might influence inclusion and the local educator's role in implementing it. The topic of state and federal mandates and their effects on local schools and teachers is an important one, and it is unfortunate that we were unable to spend more time today discussing it."

Member Check. The purpose of the member check is to provide an opportunity to verify how members feel about selected issues. Sometimes a point is given extensive discussion, and it is possible to interpret the length of the discussion as an indicator that all members feel the same way. It may, however, be that only a few members feel strongly and some have different or at least less intense feelings.

> *"Let me identify some key discussion points and then I would like to find out how each of you feel about them by checking with each member. At this point, I'm not looking for further discussion, just a general idea of how many of you feel a particular way. Again, please let me know your opinion. First, how many of you feel that it would be difficult or undesirable to have a special education teacher in your classroom for part of the school day?"*

The moderator quickly circles through all participants and secures their reaction.

> *"Second, how many of you feel that having students with mild-to-moderate disabilities in your classroom can be an advantage for that child as well as for your other students?"*

The moderator quickly circles through all participants and secures their reactions.

> *Closing Statements.* In the closing statements, the moderator has several goals. The first goal is to request that the participants keep the information stated as anonymous as possible. Second, the moderator must answer any questions and thank the participants for their assistance.

> *"As we come to a close, I need to remind each of you that the audiotape will be transcribed, you will be assigned false names for the purpose of transcript and data analysis so that you will remain anonymous, and then the tape will be destroyed. We ask that you refrain from discussing the comments of group members and that you respect the right of each member to remain anonymous. Are there any questions I can answer?"*

Thank you for your contribution to this project. This was a very successful interview and your honest and forthright responses will be an enormous asset to our work. Again, we very much appreciate your involvement."

The moderator's guide is prepared and checked by members of the research team. Further decisions in preparation for the conduct of the focus group interviews include determining the number of focus groups, the number of participants, and how best to prepare to conduct the focus groups. Questions the investigator should be prepared to address during the preparation stage for the focus group interview are provided in Table 4.2.

Number, Time, Size, and Setting of Focus Groups

Number of Focus Groups. The exact number of groups that are needed to adequately address the purpose and research questions is often difficult to predetermine. The establishment of the purpose and goal statements should, however, assist in providing a range. After the purpose and goals of the study are established, the researcher needs to carefully consider which participants are needed to best address the purpose and goals. An initial step is to brainstorm and develop a list of individuals or subgroups. Following the development of the brainstormed list, the researcher can divide it into two sections. The first section can include those who are essential to the success of the focus group, and the second section can include those who would be helpful but are not necessary. With this in mind, the number of focus groups needed can be determined in light of the resources available to conduct them.

The number of focus groups that should be conducted is based on the purpose of the study, the background information the individual researcher needs, the nature of the focus group, and the success of the first focus group. Most researchers agree that it is unwise to conduct only a single focus group. Conducting at least two focus groups with different participants allows the researcher to confirm the initial group's responses (Bortree, 1986; Buncher,

TABLE 4.2 Questions to Address Prior to Implementing a Focus Group
Interview

- Is the purpose statement clear and agreed on by all members of the
  research team?
- Have goals and outcomes for the focus group been established?
- Are the purpose and goals of the research addressable through focus groups?
- Are outcomes stated specifically enough so that it will be possible to
  evaluate the success of the focus group?
- Who is the target group from whom the most information is wanted?
- Are there any other groups from whom information would support the
  research project?
- How many focus groups are needed to adequately meet the established
  purposes and goals?
- How much time should be allowed for each focus group?
- Where is a location that is suitable and attractive to the target group?
- Are all of the technology and back-up supplies (if something does not work)
  available?
- Are the participants adequately informed about the purpose of the focus
  group, location, and expectations?
- Are all supplies ready, including food, compensation to participants, and
  forms?

1982; Goodman, 1984). Focus group interviews should be conducted until the moderator can predict the participants' responses
because they are redundant. In general, this requires between two
and four focus group interviews (Calder, 1978; Lyons, 1991;
McQuarrie & McIntyre, 1987).

Two things should be considered when selecting the number of
groups: (a) There should be a sufficient number of groups so that
the findings tend to be repetitive and no new information is obtained, and (b) there should be an adequate number of focus groups
to reflect the range of participants who need to be interviewed to
fully understand the topic. The number of groups selected is determined in part by the findings. If there is a lack of convergence on
themes or key ideas, additional focus groups need to be conducted.

The topic and goals also must be considered to determine the
optimal number of focus groups. For instance, it is possible in an
exploratory study that one or two focus group interviews would be

nt. Or, if the interest in conducting the focus group is to
rm ideas, then one focus group might be sufficient. If the
intention is to more fully understand people's opinions about an
issue, it is possible that an extended number of focus group interviews would be needed. In the initial stages of product development
or evaluation of materials or in a survey, a few focus groups are
probably adequate. Later, in a more summative stage of a program
evaluation, additional focus groups will be needed. The number of
focus groups ranges from 1 to 40, depending on the purpose. For
most research purposes, each target group should be replicated at
least once.

DID YOU KNOW THAT?

In a study conducted in Mexico, reported by Folch-Lyon
and Trost (1981), 44 focus group interviews were used to
ascertain the general public's rationale for the use and
nonuse of birth control.

Time. Focus group interviews typically last about 1.5 to 2
hours. The topic, group composition, and number of participants
all influence the length of the focus group, so the groups can range
from 1 to 3 hours within the same research study. Regardless of the
time needed, the participants should be informed about the allotted
time in advance and those time limits should be honored.

Group Size. Folch-Lyon and Trost (1981) indicate that groups
should consist of 6 to 12 persons. Fewer than 6 people may provide
an insufficient number for a stimulating dialogue, and more than
12 are too many for all participants to get a chance to express their
points of view. The optimum number is about 8 to 10 respondents
(Wells, 1974; Yoell, 1974). This range provides enough members
in the group to ensure ongoing conversation and interaction, as well
as provide an opportunity for each individual member of the group
to express unique perceptions. Furthermore, this number is appropriate for the moderator to facilitate, encourage, and respond to each

member of the group. If groups are too small, they can be dominated by one or two members or make participants feel obligated to speak. If groups are too large, they can potentially inhibit discussion and may be difficult to manage.

To ensure that the ideal number of respondents attends the focus group, we have found that it is useful to have a commitment from at least one person in addition to the ideal number. Often events occur the day of the focus group that prevent one or more members from attending. In certain circumstances when it appears that the likelihood for "no shows" is high (e.g., when individuals have to travel a long distance or when individuals have provided feedback early on that they may have difficulty attending), it is a good idea to invite two to three additional people. In the unusual situation in which all invitees arrive, include them all even if the group is slightly larger than needed.

A frequent concern is what to do when less than the desired number of subjects shows up for the focus group. Our advice is to conduct the focus group with those who have come. Usually, not more than one or two subjects will be missing from the group, and those who do attend deserve the opportunity to voice their opinions. Whether to use the data from a focus group with significantly fewer than the desired number of subjects will depend on the quality of the information obtained and the extent to which the moderator feels that the focus group was successful.

Another difficulty is when participants arrive late. We advise telling participants that the group will start on time and that it is not possible to include participants who are late. If they are only a few minutes late and could still make a contribution without disrupting the group, they should be included. Otherwise, they should be dismissed. One of the roles of the moderator's assistant is to escort late participants from the room, remind them of the rule, and provide them the same incentive as those who served in the group.

Setting. Think about settings in which you have had good conversations with your spouse, friends, or family members. What were those settings like? When you want to have an extended conversation with someone over an important topic, what are the characteristics of the setting you select? This information is relevant when you think about the setting for conducting the focus group interview. The setting provides the atmosphere and tone to facilitate members' comfort and willingness to disclose information.

The first factor to consider when selecting the setting is the size of the room. Rooms that are too big appear sterile and keep the group from benefiting from a cozy atmosphere. Rooms that are too small make people feel cramped and eager to leave.

The second factor to consider is the condition of the room. Is the room inviting? Does it appear professional yet cozy? Are the chairs comfortable? Is the room clean and well-kept, and does it provide the image desired? Is the table large enough so the entire group can be seated around it? Is it shaped so that members are not too far from each other? Members of the group are most likely to communicate with others who are seated across from them. Thus, table and chair arrangements that allow all group members equal access to each other is important. Chairs should be positioned around the table so that there is a comfortable distance between participants. The room should also be free of props and distracting items in the room or on the walls. Whatever items are in the room should be rather nondescript.

DID YOU KNOW THAT?

Distracting items affect group behavior. Mehrabian and Diamond (1971) revealed that preoccupation with a puzzle poster reduced head nodding, eye contact, and conversation within a group.

The third factor to consider is the extent to which equipment is available or can be used in the room. Focus groups are recorded in some way (either through audio, video, or both). The extent to which the room can adequately support the desired equipment needs to be considered.

TABLE 4.3 Location and Facility Considerations Prior to Focus Group Interview

- The chosen facility should be conveniently located to minimize travel time for the selected sample(s).
- The facility should have ample (free) parking for the total number of participants invited, and it should be accessible by public transportation.
- The facility should have an adequately sized room, not so large that the participants feel lost or so small that they feel cramped. The space should be adequate not only for the number of participants but also for the refreshments and any equipment that will be utilized.
- Comfortable seating should be available. Participants should preferably sit around a table at which each participant can see the other participants and the moderator.
- The room should be relatively soundproof.
- The setting should be free from interruptions.
- The room should have the capacity for using any equipment (e.g., video or audio equipment) that may be required.

The fourth factor to consider is the location. Location will affect an individual's willingness to participate. Several questions that should be addressed include the following: (a) How difficult will the site be for subjects to find? (b) Is it located near where most of the subjects live or work? (c) Is the site in a safe, well-lit area? and (d) Is there adequate parking? If the parking lot requires payment, this should be explained to subjects prior to the date of the focus group as should the procedures for compensation. Transportation issues should be discussed with each participant prior to the date of the focus group. Ideally, the site should be accessible through public transportation. Stewart and Shamdasani (1990) feel that shopping malls are ideal locations for focus groups because they are in prominent locations, easy to access, and familiar to most people.

Focus group interviews are most successful when they are conducted at a location that is viewed as a "retreat" from the usual workplace (Beck et al., 1986). Thus, for teachers, a different school would qualify as a different workplace but not as a retreat. The alumni centers or faculty clubs at some universities are often very comfortable facilities and are good examples of a "retreat" for educators. Some considerations about the location and facility that need to be made prior to conducting a focus group interview are summarized in Table 4.3.

When you select a setting for conducting the focus group, you communicate a great deal. The setting is more than just the physical environment—although that is a critical component to the success of a focus group interview. The physical setting should provide for an intimate and comfortable environment, and it should reflect an environment that will facilitate participants' responses.

The critical aspects of the environment are those that relate to the participants' backgrounds. For example, focus group interviews conducted with factory workers in an executive suite may cause discomfort and not facilitate open responses. We find that a round table with comfortable chairs placed close together provides a relaxed setting that invites everyone to contribute.

The room should be without interruptions. Arrangements should be made so that the telephone or uninformed people do not interrupt the focus group. If the focus group interview is going to be audio- or videotaped, participants should be told prior to the day of the focus group. When participants are not informed until they arrive, they do not have the option of refusing, which may make them unnecessarily anxious.

Remember that the setting establishes the importance of the focus group. The setting you select communicates to the subjects the extent to which you value their participation and their responses. Be sure that the site you select is one that participants will view positively and that will provide comfort.

ACTIVITIES

1. Select a topic of interest and identify in one or two sentences the general purpose of the focus group. Ask three people to read your purpose statement and then tell you in their own words what they think you want to know. Evaluate the quality of your purpose statement based on the extent to which the interpretation of others matches your own.

2. Using the same purpose statement that you devised in the preceding activity, make a list of what you do and do not want to know about the topic. Show this list to the same three people. Ask them if they can generate issues on the list that might be discussed at the focus group. Use these issues to determine if your *do* and *do not* lists are complete.

3. Briefly describe to several friends what a focus group is. Ask them what incentives would motivate them to agree to participate.

4. Consider settings that might be appropriate for the conduct of focus groups. Identify at least three, and evaluate them using the criteria in this chapter. See if you can find a setting that would be suitable for the conduct of a focus group.

ACTIVITIES

SELECTION OF PARTICIPANTS

OVERVIEW

This chapter addresses issues related to the identification and selection of samples. Once the purpose and goals for the focus groups are clearly established, the next step is to identify the characteristics and profile of the target subjects who should be included. The accuracy and usefulness of the information obtained from focus group interviews are directly related to the success in recruiting appropriate subjects. Identifying subjects and recruiting them to participate in the focus group interview is the single most important aspect of the success of the focus group interview. Because all of the data from the interview comes from the subjects, their accurate selection, identification, and recruitment is essential. A poorly recruited focus group or participants who are not carefully selected will doom the focus group and make it impossible to salvage.

Occasionally, it is difficult to tell who the appropriate respondents are until an initial focus group interview has been conducted. In that case, the first focus group interview serves as a pilot until the questions can be refined and the characteristics of the participants specified. Not surprisingly, there are some issues related to subject selection and recruitment that are the same as in more traditional research designs and some that are unique to focus group methodology.

CHAPTER 5

KEY IDEAS IN THIS CHAPTER

- ◆ On most occasions, group members with homogeneous characteristics should be selected.

- ◆ Description of purposive sampling and how it differs from random sampling.

- ◆ Considerations when implementing purposive sampling with focus group interviews.

- ◆ Procedures for establishing criteria for sample selection.

- ◆ A description of issues that should be considered in sample selection.

- ◆ Recruitment strategies and guidelines following sample selection.

- ◆ Procedures to prepare participants for the focus group interview.

- ◆ Factors affecting the likelihood that persons will agree to participate and attend focus groups.

Developing a Sampling Plan

Because the research goals for conducting focus groups often differ from those of quantitative research, the procedures related to selecting a sample are usually not directly applicable (Borg, Gall, & Gall, 1993). A randomly selected sample from a target group is usually the ideal sampling plan for quantitative designs. Qualitative research methods (such as focus groups), however, are designed to select members based on predetermined characteristics. If there is a large cohort of individuals who meet these predetermined characteristics, it is possible to randomly select participants from that group. Often, this is not the case. The most frequently used sampling procedure in qualitative research designs (such as focus groups) is *purposive sampling.*

Purposive Sampling. What is purposive sampling, and how is it applied to focus groups? Purposive sampling is a procedure by which researchers select a subject or subjects based on predetermined criteria about the extent to which the selected subjects could contribute to the research study. For focus groups, specific criteria that relate to the target subjects for each of the focus groups are identified based on the extent to which they are homogeneous and likely to contribute to a successful focus group. For example, a researcher may be interested in conducting focus groups with teachers who are implementing a specific instructional strategy procedure in their classroom. Subjects for the focus group might need to be restricted based on the following criteria: (a) whether the teacher is currently implementing the designated strategy, (b) the length of time the teacher has been implementing the strategy, (c) the grade level of the students, (d) descriptive criteria of the teacher (e.g., number of years experience, educational level, teaching expertise), and (e) descriptive criteria of the student (e.g., class size, socioeconomic status, linguistic ability, and achievement level). Obtaining an adequate sample that meets all of the criteria for the focus group may eliminate the possibility of obtaining a randomly selected sample.

With purposive sampling, the primary goal is not generalizability per se but understanding of an issue or topic in sufficient detail to provide information to design subsequent studies. Thus, non-probability, nonrandomly selected samples are the rule. Basch (1987) suggested that purposive sampling procedures are appropriate for focus group interviews to investigate how representative different views are and how strongly these views are held.

Although purposive sampling is the most frequently used sampling procedure, there are occasionally opportunities to select respondents randomly from stratified groups. For example, Elrod (1981) suggested that when employees are used for focus group interviews, they can be randomly selected from a specific employee category (e.g., secretary, teacher, clinical psychologist).

Considerations With Purposive Sampling. Two of the most significant potential problems with purposive sampling for focus group interviews are (a) use of convenience samples and (b) generalizability. The use of convenience samples is the least desirable approach to purposive sampling because the tendency is to rely on those subjects who are available and willing to attend with little regard to pre-identified criteria. In addition to random sampling (which is not often possible with focus groups) and convenience samples (which arc not desirable), Patton (1980) suggested five other types of samples that lend themselves to use with focus group interviews.

1. *Extreme or deviant cases:* The goal is to identify a specific subtype on which more information is needed and to identify cases that meet the criteria for that extreme group.

2. *Typical cases:* The goal is to identify those persons who most represent the group and are not outliers in any known ways.

3. *Maximum variation cases:* The goal is to identify individuals who have demonstrated unique variation in their abilities to adapt to different conditions.

4. *Critical cases:* The goal is to establish criteria to identify the most relevant (critical) cases with the intention that what is true for them will also be true for other related cases.

5. *Politically important or sensitive cases:* The goal is to address a research or evaluation question that can best be determined through including target individuals who have access to information that will enlighten the politically important or sensitive nature of the issue.

Generalizability is infrequently the goal of focus group interviews. Subsequent research designs follow up on the initial findings from focus groups and establish the generalizable findings. Because samples for focus groups are rarely randomly selected, it is not possible to make inferences from the data to a larger population due to the bias of the sample selection. Yin (1989) argues, however, that replication logic, which applies to multiple experiments, is also the same for case studies:

> If similar results are obtained from all three cases, replication is said to have taken place. This replication logic is the same whether one is repeating certain critical experiments, is limited to a few cases due to the expense or difficulty in performing a surgical preparation in animals, or is limited by the rarity of occurrence in a clinical syndrome. In each of these situations an individual case or subject is considered akin to a single experiment, and the analysis must follow cross-experiment rather than within-experiment design and logic. (p. 53)

This rationale about generalizability resulting from multiple case studies applies to the use of multiple focus groups. Thus, although generalizability may not be the goal, it is still possible to attain by conducting multiple focus groups that converge on the same findings.

Establishing Criteria for Sample Selection

Establishing the purpose of the focus group and identifying the audience lead to the development of the selection criteria for participants. Target group members should be included as participants in at least one of the focus group interviews so that their opinions are solicited.

Sampling for focus groups appears deceptively easy. Nonetheless, it requires decisions and choices that will ultimately affect the outcome of the study. Sampling for focus groups requires the establishment of *boundaries*, which limit and define the characteristics of the subjects. These boundaries for focus groups include (a) the number of participants needed, (b) the subgroups of participants needed and the extent to which they will adequately and completely address the research question, (c) whether the participants are so homogeneous that alternative points of view are not generated, (d) the extent to which selected participants will provide information that is *believable* in light of the purpose of the study, and (e) (although generalizability is not the goal) the extent to which participants will enhance generalizability.

DID YOU KNOW THAT?

Quiriconi and Dorgan (1985) have developed a model for determining the personality types of individuals based on their performance in focus groups. According to their model, there are three behavioral types:

1. *Unconventional* types are individuals who behave in a different fashion from prevailing conventions: (a) *marginalists* are those who require immediate gratification, put high emphasis on their bodies, and have limited interests in anything other than what they are focused on; (b) *loners* are more investigative and interested in the mind and thinking and tend to be more pessimistic; and (c) *literalists* are more concrete and optimistic.

2. *Conventional* types are frequently in agreement with the standards of society and its conventions: (a) *traditionalists* are past oriented and authority bound, (b) *self-achievers* are illusion builders and romantic, and (c) *trendsetters* are quantity oriented, body emphasizers, and charmers.

3. *Altruistic* types are those whose motivation is primarily to make a social contribution: (a) *intellectualizers* are abstract oriented, mind emphasizers, and methodical; (b) *self-actualizers* are introspective and integrated; and (c) *romantics* are high on intimacy and body emphasis and are emotional.

Group Membership. One of the most frequently asked questions regarding group membership is the extent to which members should be selected based on distinguishing characteristics that define them homogeneously or heterogeneously. In general, researchers suggest that participants should be selected based on predetermined characteristics that provide for a more homogeneous group. There are, however, several arguments for the selection of subjects based on heterogeneous characteristics. For example, in the case in which the questions and topic for the focus group are purely exploratory, or perhaps even speculative, it might be more effective to have a heterogeneous group with follow-up focus group interviews that are more homogeneous. For most focus group interviews, we recommend homogeneous subject selection with respect to the background, demographic, and sociocultural characteristics of the participants.

Within a particular study, it is also possible to identify characteristics of participants that are homogeneous within the focus group but heterogeneous across the study. For example, in the study conducted by Lengua et al. (1992), three focus groups were implemented. One used two-parent families, another used single- parent families, and the third used fathers. An attempt was made to maintain heterogeneity of social class and to include participants who represented high-risk families with an alcohol-abusing parent.

SUMMING UP ...

Compatibility and homogeneity are not the same thing. *Compatibility* refers to the extent to which members of the group have similar personal characteristics, interests, and acceptance of each other. *Homogeneity* refers to the characteristics of group members such as sex, age, and profession. Compatible groups are more efficient because they spend less time on group maintenance (Sapolsky, 1960) and enjoy working together more (Fry 1965; Smelser, 1961). Because most focus groups are conducted with strangers, it is unlikely that compatibility can be accurately predicted prior to the focus group.

Gender. The composition of the group by gender is of interest to researchers because the interaction styles of men and women are influenced by whether same-sex or cross-sex grouping occurs. Some researchers conduct both; others feel strongly that the best results occur with mixed-gender groups so it is unnecessary to conduct same-sex groups (Ruhe, 1978). In general, conformity is likely to be higher in mixed-gender groups (Reitan & Shaw, 1964). For same-sex groups, leadership traits are more likely to emerge, but they are easier for the moderator to control (Dyson, Godwin, & Hazelwood, 1976).

Age. Age is another characteristic that influences interaction style. Although it is not within the scope of this book to provide details, a summary of the research suggests that interruptions decrease with the age of the group members, conformity decreases after adolescence in most studies, and leadership increases with age (e.g., Chaubey, 1974; Smith, 1977). Age is sometimes an important factor in the study, and thus the age of participants is determined by the research question. For example, a researcher who is interested in how first-year clinical psychologists interpret their successes and failures would likely have a restricted age range of participants. When age is not a focus of the study, we feel that focus groups are best conducted with a mix of age ranges among adults.

Experts. Unless experts are explicitly sought for the study and the group is composed of experts, they should be avoided because they could possibly intimidate others in the group. For example, in a study about drug use, it would be a good idea to eliminate people whose backgrounds involve expertise in drugs (e.g., physicians or pharmacists). Also relevant to the participants' status is their experience with the research topic. Participants who are especially familiar with the designated topic (e.g., individuals who are privy to relevant information that other group members are not) should be given special consideration to determine if their background could place them in a position of authority that might unduly influence others in the group.

Strangers. An important question to address when selecting participants is whether they should be strangers, acquaintances, or friends. Individuals will be more inclined to be truthful and to freely disclose when they are talking with unfamiliar people who they will presumably not see again (Folch-Lyon & Trost, 1981). Thus, it is often recommended that group participants be strangers.

DID YOU KNOW THAT?

Strangers average 26 more relevant ideas than acquaintances in focus group interviews (Fern, 1982).

Screening Procedure. Thoughtful planning is required for appropriate participant selection. Adherence to identified social, economic, educational, and demographic characteristics is an important aspect of participant selection.

Researchers are encouraged to develop a screening procedure to aid in the selection of subjects (Bortree, 1986). The screening procedure should include specific questions to elicit information for determining which potential participants will be most effective. The purpose of the screening instrument should be to determine the eligibility, the demographic characteristics, and the descriptive background of each of the participants. Thus, the screening instrument aids in obtaining background information on potential participants that can be used to select participants and to later describe the sample.

Lederman (1990) identified two important considerations when screening for the target population for a focus group: establishing (a) predetermined criteria for members of the group and (b) the likelihood that participants would be willing to speak frankly to strangers about the issue.

Recruiting Participants

After the criteria for participant selection are identified and the screening instrument is designed, the next step is to recruit subjects.

Recruitment Strategies. The most desirable way to initiate recruitment is through the use of *membership lists,* which are available for purchase from organizations and corporations. These membership lists provide addresses, telephone numbers, and the initial information to begin screening participants. Of course, for these membership lists to be valuable to the research study, they need to include large numbers of members from the local area who meet the criteria for participation in the study. An advantage of the use of membership lists is that it is possible to randomly select subjects and then to telephone them using the screening instrument until an adequate number are found who meet criteria and are willing to participate.

A second way to initiate recruitment is to contact *target groups* that have large numbers of individuals who meet the criteria for the focus group and to request their assistance in identifying and contacting possible participants. Unfortunately, some organizations are reluctant to release names or feel that they do not have the time or resources to work with researchers on locating and contacting possible participants. Often research in education and psychology is conducted with students, teachers, or other key stakeholders from the schools. Schools and school districts represent a key target group, which can provide assistance in recruiting for focus groups. Because the focus group will be conducted for research purposes, it is often necessary to obtain approval from the school district office for research. Often this office can also provide assistance in identifying schools that would provide a cadre of possible participants. It is also possible to obtain support and assistance in the recruitment of subjects from the school principal, counselor, or PTA (Parent-Teacher Association) president. Suggestions for maximizing recruitment efforts in school and clinical settings are provided in Table 5.1.

A third way to recruit participants is through a *contact person* who represents the desired criteria for the study and is aware of others who also meet criteria. One example is a researcher interested in conducting a focus group with practicing social workers, counselors, and psychologists whose clients include individuals identified as child abusers. In this case, it is possible that an initial

TABLE 5.1 Pitfalls and Suggestions for Recruiting Subjects From School
and Clinical Settings

- Teachers and clinicians have infrequent access to a telephone and must
  often respond to telephone calls during a limited time. When contacting
  teachers and clinicians by telephone, be sure to leave them times and
  corresponding telephone numbers where you can be reached.
- Ask teachers and clinicians whether you may have their home telephone
  numbers and may call them in the evenings.
- Leave an evening telephone number where people can call you after 4:00
  p.m.
- Ask teachers and clinicians if they have a fax machine at the school and
  whether you may communicate with them by fax.
- Although expensive and time-consuming, an effective way to communicate
  with teachers and clinicians is to go to their schools or businesses during
  lunch, breaks, or before or after the workday to meet with them.

---

contact with one professional serving in that role would lead to the
identification of others.

A fourth way to recruit participants is through *referral from
members* of similar focus groups. Thus, if the investigator intends
to conduct several focus groups with the same subtype of individuals, it is possible that once the first focus group is identified, the
members from that group could assist in the identification of other
possible participants.

Guidelines for Recruitment. Fedder (1990) provided some guidelines to assist in recruiting participants. The first consideration is
to recruit with a professional manner and to make individuals aware
that their participation is important and valuable. Inform the
potential participants that they were carefully selected to be involved in the focus group and tell them why they were selected.
Emphasize the contribution the participants will make and how
essential it is that their point of view be obtained. Table 5.2 provides
a sample dialogue for recruiting participants, and Table 5.3 provides
a sample follow-up letter to be sent to prospective participants.

The second consideration is to be certain that all necessary
information is available before making a call. In addition, it is
important to have sufficiently role played the contact with others,

TABLE 5.2 Sample Dialogue for Recruiting Participants for Focus Group Interviews

Hello, Mr. Jones? This is Linda Elfner from the University of Miami. I would like to take just a few minutes of your time to tell you about a research study we are conducting and to solicit your help.

First, let me tell you how you were selected. We were very interested in conducting this study and including men and women who have children between ages 7 and 12 and whose children are attending one of three elementary schools in the area. You were identified through your son's classroom teacher and the school principal as a parent who might be interested in providing information to a research team on your child's homework practices.

The purpose of this study is to determine the parents' perceptions of the amount of homework their child has and the extent to which they think the homework is useful in increasing their child's learning. We also are interested in how much time parents spend with their child on homework.

You were carefully selected for participation in this study and we are very hopeful that you will agree to be part of a group of parents who will give us their opinions on these issues. What is very important is that there are no right or wrong answers, but what we are interested in is what you think and how things are going for you related to this issue. This contribution is very important because we are going to summarize the responses of more than 50 parents and to use this information to assist the school district in determining homework practices. Furthermore, the information will be provided to other agencies, such as the State Department of Education, which might find it useful in establishing homework practices. The contribution that you will make is essential to our better understanding of this important topic, and we feel that you are uniquely suited to assist us. You may have some questions, and I will do my best to answer them.

to have anticipated many of the subjects' questions, and to have prepared answers. In those few instances when questions are asked that you are unable to answer, let the participant know that you will obtain the answer as quickly as possible and return the call. If possible, do not let the unanswered question deter the participant from agreeing to be included in the focus group.

The third consideration is to cultivate a relationship in a way that communicates that you are personally benefiting and that what the participants are doing will be helpful to you and others. Specifically indicate that, although the information provided will remain anonymous, the individual's participation is extremely helpful to you personally and to the research community in a broader sense.

TABLE 5.3 Sample Follow-Up Letter for Recruiting Participants for
Focus Group Interviews

July 17, 1994

Jose Cabrerra
2300 W. 21 St.
Miami, FL 33125

Dear Jose,

Thank you for agreeing to participate in the discussion group on students'
perceptions of issues related to the roles of males and females during dating. As we
mentioned to you on the telephone, we will be conducting several of these group
discussions around the Dade County area and are quite interested in your opinion
about this topic. Following is the date, time, and location of the particular group
discussion we discussed on the telephone.

DATE: September 21, Tuesday

TIME: 6:00 p.m.

LOCATION: University of Miami Faculty Center, 2600 Red Road (269-3089)

TRANSPORTATION: Free parking is available at the center. Bus #25 stops
across the street from the center. The metrorail "university" stop is two blocks
east of the center.

REFRESHMENTS: Light dinner and soft drinks will be provided.

As we discussed on the phone, casual attire is appropriate. Also, you should expect
to be at the University of Miami Faculty Center until approximately 8:00 p.m.
Remember, it is important to arrive on time because if you arrive after the group
discussion has begun we will not be able to include you.

In order to acknowledge, in some way, your time commitment on behalf of the
University of Miami, we will give you a $25.00 gift certificate to Burdines
department store upon the completion of the discussion.

Again, thank you for your support. If you have any questions, please call Sharon
Vaughn at 290-0031.

Sincerely,

Sharon Vaughn, Ph.D.

The fourth consideration is to make the participants' time
worthwhile so that when they complete the focus group interview
they will feel that what they did was valuable. This includes
providing sincere and specific feedback about the value of the
session and the extent to which it will provide assistance to the
research project.

Preparing Participants

Participants should be informed of the general purpose (in other words, that it is a research discussion) and of the general topic. They should not be told specifically what the research questions are, nor should they be given a very clear idea of the topic lest they become too sensitized to the issue before the focus group interview. Minimal preparation—usually a general description of the topic at the time the individuals are invited—is about all that is required to prepare individuals for participation. At the time participants are invited to take part in the focus group interview, effort should be made to allay concerns and to help them feel comfortable about the focus group experience. It should also be stressed that the participants' responses will be kept confidential (Lyons, 1991), that the goal of the interview is to obtain their points of view on the topics presented, and that, therefore, no personal preparation is expected. Either prior to or during the interview, participants can be provided a permission form to obtain their informed consent. Table 5.4 is a sample permission form that was sent to prospective participants before the focus group interviews began.

There are times when it may be helpful, prior to the focus group, to provide specific examples of the kinds of questions that will be asked or a general description of the issues the individuals will be addressing. Occasionally, it is beneficial to introduce the group to potentially unfamiliar concepts that may require some reflection prior to the interview. It is important, however, to consider whether knowledge of the focus group topics prior to the interview may cause participants to enter the focus group interview with preconceived notions that may detract from spontaneous and genuine responses (Elrod, 1981).

Encouraging Attendance. People are generally willing to participate in focus group interviews, and they appear to enjoy the interviews when they do participate. Being asked their opinions, being listened to genuinely, and knowing that their opinions are anonymous and that their input will influence a decision or goal appear to be valuable experiences for many people (Bennett, 1986).

TABLE 5.4 Sample Permission Form

Dear Parents,

I would like to invite you to take part in a study being conducted by the University of Miami. This study is being conducted in an effort to better understand how Hispanic parents assist their children with reading and writing at home and what schools can do to assist the parents in this endeavor. Part of this study will include a brief interview with a group of concerned parents such as yourself.

This group of concerned parents will be interviewed for 1 hour at South Miami Heights Elementary School. All those who participate will be reimbursed for their time. Each family will receive a $10 gift certificate for Foodline Supermarket. In addition, refreshments will be served at the interview, and child care will be provided for children under 8 years of age.

What is said during this interview will be kept confidential to the extent permitted by law, with no parent or student names being used in reporting the results. All information linking parent and student names to this study will be destroyed once the study has been completed.

I believe you will be a valuable contributor to the group, and I would like to include you in this study. To participate, just sign the consent form below and return it to your child's teacher before Thursday, January 13. I will send home a letter with your child before the day of the interview telling you in which room we will be meeting.

If you have any questions about this study, you may contact Marie Hughes at the University of Miami, 248-5164. Thank you for your cooperation.

Sincerely,

Marie Tejero Hughes, M.S.Ed.

INFORMED CONSENT

Please check one of the following:

_____Yes, I am willing to participate in the study described above concerning Hispanic parents' assistance with their children's reading and writing at home.

Which interview date can you attend? Check one:

_____Friday, January 14 at 3:00 p.m.
_____Tuesday January 18 at 7:00 p.m.
_____No, I am not able to participate in this study.

_____   _____
Parent's signature   Date

Please print:

_____   _____
Name of parent or guardian   Name of student

_____   _____
Telephone number   Teacher's name

PLEASE RETURN THIS FORM TO YOUR CHILD'S TEACHER

DID YOU KNOW THAT?

After participating in focus group interviews, individuals often feel a higher level of commitment and motivation because the focus group served as a sign that the "powers that be" cared about the participants and were interested in their experiences, thoughts, and feelings (Basch, 1987; Elrod, 1981). This may be of great benefit in educational research where the voices of teachers, students, and parents are often thought to be muffled (Johnston & Crawford, 1989).

Perhaps of most importance in securing consent and attendance from participants is the selection of a date and time when they can attend. Although it is difficult to organize a date and time that is equally convenient for all members of the focus group, effort should be made to represent the interests of all participants. The best procedure is to select a 2-week period of time when you would like to conduct the focus group. Be certain that the period selected is at least 3 weeks away from when you will be contacting subjects. Ask each subject to provide you with 5 days and blocks of times on those days when it would be possible to attend the focus group. Prioritize the 5 days and times, and assure each subject that you will contact each of them and do all that you can to select a day and time that is one of their highest priorities. Be sure to consider special events and religious holidays before selecting a date.

Refreshments, snacks, and beverages are integral to establishing an atmosphere for interaction. Individuals participating in the focus group should be informed in advance of the type of refreshments to be served. For example, light snacks, lunch, cheese, and fruit are appropriate. Beverages can include coffee, tea, and soft drinks; under no circumstances should alcoholic beverages be served at a focus group. It is also helpful to inform participants that the food and beverages are available prior to the focus group and can be taken to their places at the table. For focus groups extending beyond 1 hour and 30 minutes, participants should be provided with a break of a few minutes to obtain additional refreshments and to use the rest rooms.

People who are outgoing and enjoy meeting and talking with others are much more likely to accept participation in a focus group than individuals who are reluctant communicators. For this reason, *it is preferable to provide incentives for participants.* Otherwise, the findings could be biased to reflect those people who enjoy group participation. Bers (1987) suggests that if funds to pay participants are difficult to obtain, they should be justified as part of the essential cost of conducting research, much in the same way as printing and postage costs are necessary to a mail survey. Typically, the reimbursement to participants of focus groups is related to their salaries (Beck et al., 1986), and the amounts suggested range from $20 to $100. Individuals who have not previously participated in focus groups and are unfamiliar with the approach are the most difficult to recruit, and, therefore, *it is essential that they too be paid.* The guidelines for encouraging attendance and participant preparation are outlined in Table 5.5.

DID YOU KNOW THAT?

Krueger (1988) has established a three-level system for reimbursing participants for their participation in focus groups.

Level I ($15 to $25): Individuals who are easy to locate and willing to participate.

Level II ($25 to $50): Individuals who must meet several criteria for selection or who have moderate amounts of conflicts in their schedules.

Level III ($75 to $100+): Individuals who must meet precise criteria, who are underrepresented in the community, or who have high amounts of conflicts in their schedules.

TABLE 5.5 Guidelines for Encouraging Attendance and Participant Preparation

- Provide participants with a letter prior to the focus group interview that informs them of the time and location (with directions) of the interview and of the value of the role they are playing. Telephone confirmation of the date and time of the focus group interview should also be provided.
- Participants should be informed in advance that there will be some cash incentive or gift certificate provided to participants at the close of the focus group interview.
- Food and drink (nonalcoholic) provide encouragement for attendance and also are essential to the success of the focus group interview.
- Participants should be informed in advance that latecomers will not be allowed to participate because of the disruption to the group.
- A certificate of completion of attendance in the focus group can be awarded at the end of the interview.

ACTIVITIES

1. Identify the characteristics of purposive sampling and random sampling. Compare and contrast these two approaches. Identify the major strength of each of the sampling approaches.

2. Purposive sampling is best applied to one of the following research cases: (a) when extreme or deviant cases are of interest, (b) to illustrate typical cases, (c) to investigate maximum variation, (d) to examine critical cases, and (e) to include politically important or sensitive cases. Select one of these five cases and do the following: (a) Write the general purpose of the study, (b) identify at least one research question, and (c) specify the sample selection criteria that will correspond with the case you selected.

3. Develop a telephone recruitment procedure for the study you designed in Activity 2. Ask *a friend* if you can call him or her and try out your recruitment strategy. If you have a recorder on your telephone, ask your friend if you may record the conversation so that you can evaluate your performance. Ask your friend for feedback on your performance. Listen to the tape and evaluate your success.

4. Provide one example of a research study that would benefit from including a heterogeneous group for the focus group. Provide another example of a research study that would benefit from including a homogeneous group for the focus group.

ROLE OF THE MODERATOR

OVERVIEW

The role of the moderator is central to a successful focus group interview. This is due to the fact that the functions performed by the moderator are inextricably linked to each aspect of the focus group (e.g., Cohen & Engleberg, 1989; Gordon, 1990; Ringo, 1992). For example, even before the focus group interview is conducted, the moderator is frequently involved in developing a moderator's guide, including questions and probes to be used during the focus group interview. The moderator may also be involved in contacting and recruiting possible participants and in arranging for the focus group facility. Also, just prior to the initiation of the focus group interview itself, the moderator is active in creating an environment that will facilitate open and honest participation by focus group members. It is, however, the moderator's primary responsibility to ensure that the respondents' answers meet the purpose of the focus group interview. In so doing, the moderator must be cognizant not only of the goal of the focus group interview but also of the appropriate verbal and nonverbal techniques for facilitating honest and spontaneous responses on the topic. The moderator has special insight into the techniques used to elicit subject participation, the climate of the discussion, and the tone and intent behind particular responses. All of these are vital in data analysis and interpretation.

Although the responsibilities of the moderator are quite varied, the clearer the moderator's understanding of the research question, the better able he or she will be to meet those responsibilities.

CHAPTER 6

KEY IDEAS IN THIS CHAPTER

◆ The moderator is involved in much more than just the group component of the focus group interview. The various related functions of the moderator are presented in this chapter with special emphasis given to the moderator's role within the focus group discussion.

◆ There are special methods of communication used by moderators to encourage and direct the focus group discussion. These techniques are described.

◆ Moderators may inhibit or negatively influence participants' responses in overt and subtle ways. Examples of these pitfalls are presented along with potential solutions.

The Moderator's Role
Within the Focus Group Interview

PLANNING FOR THE FOCUS GROUP

Initially the moderator must fully understand the objectives of the study. An incomplete understanding of the objectives cannot be adjusted for in the final analysis, as is sometimes possible with other research techniques. Although the focus group interview itself may be recorded or even viewed live by vested parties, it is the moderator alone who works directly with the group and guides the participants' discussion. Therefore, the moderator must know before beginning what information will be useful to the researchers.

For example, a moderator who allows participants to spend considerable time discussing their personal experiences at counseling facilities *off campus* when the focus group is concerned with the attitudes of college students toward the counseling services available *on campus* is collecting interesting but unusable data. A moderator who allows participants to spend time on information that is tangential or unrelated to the study decreases the time available for discussing information that is appropriate and necessary.

The moderator must also understand what information is desired and how this information can best be obtained. It is important that the moderator discern *prior* to the focus group interview whether the immediate goal is to obtain information on the participants' (a) past behaviors, thoughts, or feelings; (b) current behaviors, thoughts, or feelings; or (c) future or ideal behaviors, thoughts, or feelings. In the preceding example, the researchers may have been interested in the participants' overall feelings toward their campus counseling facility (e.g., how effective the facility was in meeting their needs) or their specific experiences with particular aspects of the facility (e.g., their impressions about their relationships with their therapists, the physical structure of the facility, or specific changes the participants would recommend for different areas of the facility). The researchers also may have been interested in the participants' expectations prior to entering counseling compared with their actual experiences once in counseling.

In another illustration, the researchers were interested in students' perceptions of their field experience for their master's degree programs in special education. As a result, focus groups were conducted where the main area of interest was the students' experiences in their field placements. At the end of a study examining the type of planning teachers engage in to meet the needs of their mainstreamed students, focus groups were conducted with elementary school teachers to discover what changes they would suggest if the study were to be conducted in the future (Schumm, Vaughn, Haager, et al., 1995).

INTRODUCTIONS

The moderator is often the only individual to meet the participants when they arrive. The moderator greets the participants and makes introductions. In doing this, no professional titles (e.g., doctor, president) should be used. This serves to maintain equality between the moderator and the participants and limit any undue influence the moderator's title may have on the participants' responses. For example, when people see a white lab coat, they tend to assume that the individual donning the coat is an expert. Likewise, if the moderator is introduced as *Dr.* while the participants are referred to by their first names or by *Mr.* and *Ms.*, a similar effect may occur. If the participants believe the moderator is in a one-up position, their responses may not be as free as if the moderator was viewed as an equal. Furthermore, using only first names humanizes the moderator so that the participants will want to speak freely and genuinely. In general, the moderator must be wary of intimidating the participants, particularly at this introductory stage.

If other interested parties are going to be viewing the focus group interview (e.g., from behind a one-way mirror), it is beneficial that they *not* be introduced to the participants. The participants will, however, need to be made aware of the general fact that the focus group *interview* (taking the emphasis off of the participants) is being viewed. The reason for not introducing these individuals is the same as that for not introducing the moderator by his or her professional title. Some participants may become uncomfortable or intimidated if aware that professionals or individuals with vested interests in the focus group outcome are going to be watching. For others, just knowing the faces of the individuals who will be watching is discomforting.

It is important to note that the ethical guidelines concerning the use of human subjects apply to participants in focus group interviews. If an adverse consequence may result from the observation of a participant in a focus group, the participant must be made aware of this possibility and given the option of declining participation. Imagine the scenario in which the dean of a college is watching a focus group of faculty members who teach within the dean's college. If the participants are informed that the focus group interview will be viewed, they are likely to assume the viewing will be anonymous.

OPENING THE DISCUSSION

Once the participants have arrived, it is up to the moderator to collect demographic information on the participants for consideration later in the analyses and to complete and distribute name tags to the participants. Again, it is preferable to omit titles from name tags and for the moderator, participants, and other involved individuals to refer to each other by *first names* so that an equal status is afforded to all. The moderator then serves as the congenial host, introducing the participants to each other, inviting them to help themselves to refreshments, pointing out rest room locations, informing participants of any special regulations (e.g., whether smoking is allowed in the facility), as well as settling participants for the initiation of the interview.

Once the moderator is ready to begin the discussion, the roles of both the moderator and the participants in the focus group interview must be more clearly defined. At this point, the moderator discusses the components included in the introduction section of the moderator's guide. For example, the moderator may explain that the purpose of the interviews is to learn about the specified topic from the participants and that questions will be asked to fully understand what each participant is saying. It is important at this point to stress that there are no wrong answers nor ideal responses and that everyone's participation is valued. The moderator may add more specific recommendations depending upon the group (e.g., the importance of repeating a point that has already been made in order to gain everyone's point of view on the topic and that verbalizing contradictory points of view is both acceptable and expected). In the process of introducing the interview topic, it is important that the moderator clarify any difficult or novel concepts and jargon and describe the level of confidentiality to be maintained throughout the study. The introduction sets the tone for the remainder of the interview, and it is important that the participants be put at ease as soon as possible. Table 6.1 lists comments and issues that should be included in the moderator's opening remarks. In addition, the warm-up questions or exercises, which follow the introduction and are included in the moderator's guide, will also help make the participants feel relaxed. (See Chapter 4 for a discussion of the components of the moderator's guide.)

CREATING AND MAINTAINING A COMFORTABLE ENVIRONMENT

A supportive and nonevaluative environment must be established if the subjects are to participate honestly and freely. The development of such an environment begins by maximizing the comfort of the participants. For example, it is recommended that refreshments (including coffee but excluding liquor) be available before, during, and after the focus group interview. The availability of refreshments often promotes recruitment and serves as an ice-breaker once at the focus group site. Simple and easily handled foods such as chips and cold finger sandwiches work best: Crunchy foods are not advisable if the session is to be audiotaped.

It is also the responsibility of the moderator to ensure that the refreshments are prepared, delivered, and set up at the focus group site before the arrival of the participants. When focus group participants are adults, it is often preferable to allow them to access refreshments, beverages, and the rest rooms. Participants are more comfortable when they are in charge of their own needs rather than having to ask permission of others (e.g., to leave the room). This

TABLE 6.1 Contents for the Moderator's Opening Remarks

- A welcoming statement that thanks the participants for their time and assistance.
- A description of where the refreshments and rest rooms are located and whether participants will be able to move about or leave the room (e.g., in order to get refreshments or use the rest rooms) during the focus group interview.
- An introduction of the moderator (and his or her functions) and an introduction of who is conducting the research (e.g., a departmental affiliation, or agency).
- A description of the recording techniques to be used and whether observers are viewing the interview. (Permission for recording should be obtained at the same time the demographic questionnaire is completed.)
- A definition of a focus group and the purpose of the current group. (Be careful not to give too much information or the type of information that may influence the participants' responses.)
- An introduction of the focus group topic including definitions and explanations of difficult or novel terminology and concepts. (Be careful not to unduly influence or bias the participants.)
- A disclaimer relaying that the moderator has no vested interests in the particular outcome of the focus group.
- A statement describing confidentiality.
- A statement stressing that there are no wrong answers and relaying the importance of each individual's responses, including repeated and contradictory ideas.
- A statement about the types of information wanted.
- Introductions by the participants of their first names.

---

also provides the least disruption to the focus group interview itself. In addition, any equipment that is going to be used (e.g., video or tape recorders) must also be set up and ready prior to the participants' arrivals. When recordings are used, special permission of the participants is required.

Even such specific and seemingly trivial details as the seating arrangement must be taken into consideration and thoughtfully arranged before the participants arrive. Also important is the facility itself. A dirty or odorous room will, almost undoubtedly, cause discomfort. (See Chapter 4 for a detailed description of the necessary facility for conducting focus group interviews.) Keep in mind that the pre-interview environment will likely set the tone for the rest of the day. If participants arrive and there are still details to be taken care of, then full attention cannot be placed on the participants. As a result, they will likely view the moderator as hasty and slipshod, rather than competent and in control.

A moderator may establish and maintain a comfortable environment through the choice of words. A moderator who verbally separates him- or herself from the group may literally be isolating the participants. Moderators should try to keep the participants' attention on the group rather than on the moderator. For example, "now let's talk about . . ." is more focused on the group as one entity than, "now I would like to talk about . . ." The latter form disqualifies the needs and importance of the participants and places the moderator in a more commanding position (National Association for Independent Colleges and Universities, 1991, p. 14). Also, people like to know that they are doing a good job. Moderators can calm participants' performance concerns and improve participation by providing positive feedback and praise (e.g., "This group is going very well."). Whenever in doubt, the moderator can consider the position of the participant (e.g., "Would I feel comfortable and secure enough to freely speak my mind at this moment?").

CONTROLLING THE TOPIC

The focus group discussion serves as the data source, and there are no second chances with focus groups. Once the moderator ends the focus group discussion and the participants leave the interview, the moderator cannot later contact a participant to clarify a response. The moderator must, therefore, gain the information within the boundaries of the focus group interview. As with other interview methodologies, there exists a number of techniques (borrowed from psychology and communication) to facilitate the moderator in obtaining complete and accurate responses from the participants.

It is recommended that moderators begin with *more general* questions before inquiring about specific areas. It is important that the moderator's statements communicate genuine interest in the individuals' responses and that questions not be posed as a test or assessment. As a result, open-ended questions that do not suggest a "correct" answer should be used instead of close-ended questions.

For example, "What do you think of heterogeneous grouping?" is a general and open-ended question. Conversely, "In your classroom, which practice do you prefer, homogeneous or heterogeneous grouping for reading instruction?" is an example of a specific and closed question. The former question allows participants to respond more freely and in accordance with their own experience. The moderator's use of the latter, more rigid question limits the respondents' answers to one of two prechosen responses, which may be artificial for the participant. These externally created responses will likely fail to capture the full character of the respondents' own personal experience. In fact, this latter question may be interpreted as somewhat threatening. Whenever respondents have to select from prechosen answers, there may be the belief that one answer is more correct than the others. This places undue pressure on respondents, particularly in a group setting.

Once participants begin interacting, it is frequently necessary for the moderator to probe. *Probes* are invitations to expand on previous statements so responses are more specifically and fully revealed. An example of a probe would be, "John, you've mentioned that you believe mainstreaming has some negative effects on children with learning disabilities. What kind of effects are you seeing in your school?" Probes may also be directed at participants to increase their involvement (e.g., "Lori, we haven't heard your opinion about Prozac."). Probes are also used to clarify concepts and responses. When a participant says, "I feel very strongly about this," the moderator can probe to determine exactly what the participant means by "strongly." A moderator should be wary of vague responses (which possess a myriad of interpretations) and should probe for clarifying statements.

When using probes, however, it is important for the moderator not to lead the respondents or to appear aggressive or intimidating. The purpose of probing is to elicit genuine and complete answers.

Despite the intentional nature of the probing process, moderators are not always directive. Once a topic has been introduced, it is desirable that the respondents carry on the discussion with little interruption from the moderator. Moderators can even use silence (with perhaps occasional nodding) to encourage the group to continue on their own. When the respondents move off of the specified topic or when the group or specific group members require a push, the moderator becomes more interactive, providing guidelines and direction. Thus, the role of the moderator is far from static. Moderators who keep the following questions in mind will be better able to judge how successfully the focus group is running: (a) Am I obtaining the information that I need? (b) Am I addressing the questions of interest? and (c) Am I promoting the comfort and interaction of all of the group members?

When the participants' conversation moves away from the topic, it is the moderator's responsibility to guide the conversation. Often, this can be done by simply redirecting the conversation (e.g., "Let's get back to discussing the question that relates to . . .").

In addition to guarding against fluctuations in topic, the moderator must also look for respondent characteristics and behaviors that could jeopardize the cohesion of the focus group interview. The moderator needs to control any type of destructive intimidation or domination and to manage anyone attempting to serve in the role of the authority figure. For instance, it is not uncommon for an individual to monopolize a group. This type of participant is often referred to as the genuine or pseudo expert (Wells, 1974). *Genuine experts* know an exceeding amount about the topic and may intimidate others into silence. *Pseudo experts* annoy others by acting as though they know a lot about the topic. When an individual is pontificating or relaying personal experiences that do not relate directly to the question, the moderator may need to suspend such discussion and then redirect the question to others in the group. Possibly, the moderator will need to develop a new question or move on to a new topic (Bers, 1987) (e.g., "Although this has been interesting, we need to consider another question."). With the genuine expert, the moderator may need to recognize the expertise but emphasize the importance of obtaining the perspectives of all. This will also reassure the other participants that the moderator is concerned with genuine answers and not necessarily the most eloquent or technical answers.

Langer (1992) has extrapolated a number of different techniques moderators may use to curtail excessively verbose participants. The more frequently used methods are

1. placing a hand up in a stop position,
2. refraining from making eye contact with talkative participant,
3. patting the individual on the back or arm,
4. summarizing the individual's responses,
5. letting other participants know you cannot hear them when someone is speaking at the same time,
6. reminding participants that the tape cannot pick up the responses of individuals who speak at the same time, and
7. reseating the participants.

The moderator must occasionally make comments or bridge comments made by other participants to summarize and refocus the group. If group members are speaking only to the moderator, the moderator can invite a person to comment on a point made by the other person and then encourage that person to reflect or comment in return.

An uninvolved group member is a particular challenge to a moderator. The uninvolved participant may simply be quiet or may display body language that signals a lack of interest or an unwillingness to participate. To encourage quiet or withdrawn group members, it is often helpful to use a *polling technique* of eliciting each participant's feelings about a particular issue (Bellenger et al., 1976). The moderator should, however, avoid serial questioning (asking each participant to comment in the same order on every issue), which minimizes group interaction and creates a sterile environment.

The moderator may also use his or her own body language to influence the group. For example, the moderator may make eye contact with members of the group who are not participating in order to encourage participation, or the moderator may withdraw his or her eye contact in order to discourage an overly verbose participant. Another common technique includes leaning toward an individual to show greater interest and to encourage more talking (leaning away from someone has the opposite effect). Likewise, the moderator may use the body language of the participants to get them more involved in the group. For instance, a moderator may remark on body posture (e.g., "Peter, I noticed you turned away when Jorge talked about full inclusion. What is your opinion on full inclusion?") or facial expressions of participants (e.g., "Paul, you look like you may have something to add to Max's statement."). Moderators who are aware of their verbal and nonverbal messages and those of the participants will best be able to maximize the potential of the focus group dynamic. Examples are presented in Table 6.2 of how one moderator used probes and kept a focus group interview discussion on target.

ENDING THE FOCUS GROUP INTERVIEW

It is important that the moderator not allow the discussion to extend beyond its scheduled ending time. Before the end of the discussion, the moderator may wish to summarize the main points presented in the focus group, to ask for a final opinion on a particular issue, or to allow participants to express their final thoughts on the focus group in general. Points to be included in the conclusion of the focus group interview may be outlined in the wrap-up section of the moderator's guide. (See Chapter 4 for a sample wrap-up.)

Characteristics of an Effective Moderator

Although the moderator needs to have a thorough under-standing of the research topic, the moderator should not come across as an expert in the area. After all, the purpose of the focus group is to gather the knowledge of the *participants*. If the subjects believe the moderator already has mastery of the topic, they may be reluctant to share their own opinions. In fact, the moderator's

TABLE 6.2 Excerpts From a Focus Group Interview (Birnie, 1988)

Moderator directly asks for clarification through examples:

Tara: *Sensitivity, but I'm not sure if that's just a philosophy of education. I think that really belongs to a lot of people in a lot of ways. I think it keeps evolving and changing with what I do. You know, in some years I'll throw something out.*

Moderator: *Give us an example of that, Tara.*

Tara: *Something that very specifically changed: I felt I had to teach the kids everything I knew.*

Moderator: *Right, let me ask you to elaborate just a little bit, Tara.*

Tara: *I can remember one kid in my class by the name of Johnny . . .*

Moderator invites a specific individual to participate:

Sue: *. . . The most you can give.*

Moderator: *Thank you very much, Sue. Martha, would you like to go next?*

Moderator gains clarification through further questioning:

Matt: *I've been teaching for 20 years.*

Moderator: *Would you say that it's more important now with kids to provide that role model for them than it was when you first started teaching?*

Matt: *Absolutely. I always took the opportunity . . .*

Moderator brings discussion back to the central topic:

Lyn: *I would have gotten my master's. I've taken so many courses. Now I realize I'm coming back, but I figure at this point—the only thing it probably makes a difference to is moving up.*

Moderator: *But, you stayed in courses and that's what has kept you abreast of the recent research?*

Moderator checks for agreement or diversity in group opinions:

Tom: *Whatever skill I'm teaching, the first written assignment or the first exam, I plan so that nobody can fail.*

Moderator: *Would you all agree with Tom about that? About the need for children to succeed?*

Moderator comments on nonverbal behavior to encourage participation:

Moderator: *Terry, I see you are nodding.*

Terry: *Yes, I ensure student achievement . . .*

Moderator summarizes participants' statements on an issue:

Moderator: *What I think I'm hearing you all say, then, is that you don't have too many failures. You don't have too many kids who fail. Is that what you're all saying?*

Moderator connecting statements of different participants:

Perry: *I can have a kid who fails, because I don't think every kid can pass a class. I'm not that idealistic. But there's something of value in that kid anyway.*

Moderator: *That's what you were touching on earlier, wasn't it, Tiffany?*

presentation of an incomplete comprehension can be a tool to encourage participants to express their own opinions and experiences in an attempt to educate the moderator (Greenbaum, 1991a). Individuals who have good social and interviewing skills and who are sensitive and responsive to individuals in a group make effective focus group interviewers. Ideally, the moderator will be clearly in control yet approachable to the participants. In addition, the moderator should be a good listener, conveying sincere interest in the participants' responses. A good memory is also a necessity in order to connect past responses with future replies and probes. As previously stated, moderators must be capable of drawing out the more quiet participants and keeping more vocal participants from dominating the group while always promoting an environment of open exchange. Finally, the moderator will be required to record key insights and to develop a final report (for which writing skills are beneficial).

It is important to note that the personal characteristics of the moderator may influence responses. Consider whether the sex, age, or race (or combinations of these) of the moderator may facilitate or hinder honest responses from the participants. For example, what impact would a female moderator have on the responses of male sex offenders in a focus group examining the participants' experiences in therapy? Participants may consider moderators from different cultural groups or of the opposite sex as outsiders in whose presence the participants may be more inhibited and cautious in their responses. A list of the most important moderator characteristics and related skills is provided in Table 6.3.

Potential Pitfalls for the Moderator

For the responses of all the participants to be equally valued and accurately represented in the analyses, the moderator must enter each focus group relatively free of biases or preconceived notions pertaining to the focus group topic. Moderators, of course, have their own beliefs and values. It is not possible for moderators to become totally objective or to leave their own histories outside of the focus group room. Instead, effective moderators are required to

TABLE 6.3 Moderator Characteristics/Skills

- Knows about the topic but does not appear to be so all-knowing that the participants are intimidated.
- Demonstrates genuine incomplete understanding of the perceptions and attitudes of participants so that more elaborate, in-depth responses can be elicited.
- Controls the group and is clearly the leader but remains approachable and friendly.
- Leads rather than guides.
- Functions as a facilitator, not a performer.
- Possesses a good memory so that he or she can remember what the participants said and can connect it with future responses and probes.
- Listens actively and willingly.
- Is responsive to participants and does not follow preconceived ideas or adhere rigidly to the moderator's guide.
- Reacts with concern to the feelings and issues that each member states.
- Does not alienate any member of the group.
- Draws out shy or less participating members and does not allow members to dominate.
- Becomes totally involved in the interview and encourages others to remain interested, active participants.
- Possesses strong writing skills to record key insights and to write summaries, reports, and interpretations.

be highly self-aware. By outwardly acknowledging any preconceived notions and by constantly self-monitoring their own verbal and nonverbal behaviors, moderators are best able to check for instances in which their own prejudices influenced the group's, or a particular member's, responses. For example, biases based on race, sex, or social class will be destructive to the focus group and may lead to the alienation of certain participants.

Moderators who have something to gain by reaching a particular focus group outcome or who preach a personal agenda that may be supported by a particular focus group outcome will make poor moderators, despite their best intentions. Such individuals may enter into the focus group discussion believing they are capable of being impartial to views opposing their own, but moderators can influence focus group participants in very subtle ways, which may

TABLE 6.4 Questions to Ask of a Prospective Moderator

- What is your training in education, psychology, and communication?
- What training have you had in conducting groups?
- What kind of techniques do you use in a focus group interview?
- What specific experiences have you had with focus groups?
- Have you done any work in the area of *this* research project?
- Have you worked with the type of participant used in this project before?
- What would you want to know from me in order to conduct these focus groups successfully (Gordon, 1990)?
- What kind of preparation do you do in advance (Greenbaum, 1991b)?
- What do you include in your moderator guide?
- How do you describe the role you would play as the moderator in this particular focus group interview research project?

---

go undetected (e.g., by lack of eye contact to discourage a participant from verbalizing an unwelcome point of view).

Whenever the possibility exists of there being a clash between the personal interests of the moderator and objectivity in the focus group discussion, it is best to reduce the risk of moderator contamination and to use an *outside moderator*. This is an individual who has no vested interests in the outcome of the focus group interviews and, usually, is only involved in that part of the research project involving the focus groups (e.g., not in putting the results into practice). Ideally, researchers would be able to shop around for the best moderator available. Table 6.4 provides some sample questions to ask a prospective moderator. The reality of research projects, however, often mandates that the moderator be a member of the research team and not a hired consultant. The obvious confines of money and time can themselves preclude the use of an outside moderator. Using a moderator who is already part of the research team can, however, have benefits. For example, the moderator will already possess an intricate understanding of the research project and of the specific area under investigation. Whether the moderator is from the research team or not, there exist several conditions under which bias may occur.

DID YOU KNOW THAT?

Professional moderators are now available through businesses that also rent out their facilities specifically for conducting focus group interviews. These businesses will be advertised in city telephone books under such headings as *Market Research and Analysis* and in advertisements in related professional journals.

Bias may occur, for example, when the moderator is aware of the ultimate objective of the study or is too close to the actual researchers. In such cases, the moderator may inadvertently or even purposefully influence the focus group dialogue or the final report to please the researchers. In the same vein, moderators may become too close to the focus group participants. When the moderator and participants are too close, the moderator may overtly or inadvertently reveal the study objectives or the moderator's own bias to the participants. In these situations, the participants may feel a need to please the moderator by saying what they believe the moderator wants to hear (rather than what the participant is really feeling, thinking, or experiencing). Bias may also become apparent when multiple focus groups are conducted by the same moderator. In this situation, the moderator may influence a later group so their responses in the interview or as represented in the analyses are consistent with earlier groups. In order to minimize the influence of the moderator's beliefs, attitudes, and expectations on the data collection, analysis, and interpretation, it is imperative that the moderator be aware of any subjective tendencies.

Overall, moderators have a purposeful impact on the focus group interview when they encourage group discussions, discourage prohibitive or extraneous discussions, shift the talk to a particular topic, or probe to gather a greater understanding of participants' responses. Such directive work on the part of the moderator is necessary if the focus group is to yield the desired data. There is, however, the danger of the moderator exerting too much influence over the participants and thereby inhibiting the participants' free expression. Table 6.5 lists some of the more common moderator pitfalls.

TABLE 6.5 Moderator Pitfalls

- Relaying too much information at the introduction of the focus group interview such that the participants pick up on the researchers' or moderator's personal preferences concerning the project's outcome.
- Being too passive such that the focus group lacks guidance.
- Being too controlling such that the moderator inhibits the spontaneous participation and genuine responses of the participants.
- Promoting the participation of the participants unequally.
- Paying more attention to some participants than to others.
- Becoming too close to the participants so they try to please the moderator instead of giving genuine responses.
- Treating participants' conflicting points of view unequally.
- Failing to probe when participant responses could be interpreted in more than one way.
- Failing to try numerous probes when initial attempts at clarification are insufficient.
- Stopping the discussion on a particular topic after only a few of the participants have responded.
- Failing to recognize the ways in which his or her own mannerisms may be inhibiting the free participation of all the participants.
- Spending too much interview time on extraneous topics.
- Judging the success of the focus group interview on the quantity of the group interaction instead of on the quality.

Training the Moderator

After reading about the characteristics and responsibilities of the moderator, one may wonder whether anyone can adequately fill such a role. Our experience is that individuals with good social, leadership, and interviewing skills and who are sensitive and responsive to individuals in a group make effective interviewers.

If a professional moderator or an individual with extensive experience in conducting focus group interviews is used, then the only real training necessary is (as previously stated) to make the moderator thoroughly aware of the research questions and the intended objectives of the focus group interview. This includes acquainting the moderator with the types of information from the focus group participants that are going to be valuable in the final analyses. (See the first section of this chapter for specific types of information that can be gained through focus group interviews.)

When the moderator has had little or no experience with focus groups, then the best training is for the neophyte moderator to (a) observe live or videotaped focus groups conducted by experienced moderators, (b) listen to audiotapes of previously conducted focus groups, and (c) read transcripts (including moderator and participant comments) of actual focus groups. It is also advisable that the new moderator read the reports and summaries—and, if available, the moderator guides—of more experienced moderators. Transcripts and even tapes of focus groups may be available from the authors of focus group publications and from local businesses who rent out their facilities and personnel for focus group interviews. It may be beneficial for an inexperienced moderator to conduct a series of informal focus groups. For example, the moderator can practice when pretesting the moderator's guide. In sum, the best training for a new moderator is through observing the focus groups of more experienced moderators and through hands-on experience with practice focus groups.

DID YOU KNOW THAT?

A 12-hour moderator training program has been initiated at Prince George's Community College (Cohen & Engleberg, 1989). Only individuals who have successfully completed this program are used as moderators in the school's research studies. The training program focuses on the following five skills:

1. group process (e.g., norm development, group environment),
2. group leadership skills (e.g., techniques for facilitating group discussion),
3. communication skills (e.g., nonverbal communication, language usage),
4. moderator guide preparation (e.g., agenda development), and
5. report writing (e.g., summarizing, analyzing).

TABLE 6.6 Possible Responsibilities of a Moderator Aide (Birnie, 1988)

- Arrange furniture in room to accommodate participants, interviewer, and aide.
- Check room temperature and lighting and make adjustments if necessary.
- Prepare and set out refreshments.
- Set up and test equipment.
- Greet arriving participants and offer refreshments.
- Be available to moderator in order to assist with last minute details.
- Help seat participants if necessary.
- Operate equipment during focus group interview.
- Take notes during focus group interview.
- Help participants exit building.
- Review session with moderator and research team if desired.
- Help clean up focus group area and put away equipment.

Moderator Aide

Many large-scale research projects, particularly university-based studies, will require a moderator aide. As the name denotes, this individual (usually a graduate assistant) assists with the moderator's duties. Just prior to the start of a focus group interview, there are many things that need to be accomplished (e.g., setting up refreshments, passing out name tags, checking equipment, making introductions), and the moderator working alone may have a difficult time completing everything on time and in a professional manner. The qualifications of the moderator aide will vary according to the particular research study and research team and the requisite needs of each. A moderator aide whose primary responsibilities are to check equipment and set up refreshments needs minimal credentials. A moderator aide who is expected to contribute to the more complex steps of the study (e.g., data analysis) will, however, need demonstrated proficiency in that specific activity. Table 6.6 is a list of possible responsibilities that may be delegated to a moderator aide.

ACTIVITIES

1. Conduct a mock focus group with a few friends in which you fulfill the role of the moderator. Practice using the various probes described in this chapter. What effects did the different probes have on the group participants and their discussion? Which probes worked best for you and why?

2. Develop a study question (or questions) for which you would use focus group interviews. Based on your research question(s) and the subjects you would be interested in studying, which moderator characteristics would have a negative impact on the free expression of the participants? Which moderator characteristics may actually enhance the productivity and honesty of the group?

3. Interview a professional moderator. Ask specific questions about his or her training and experiences. Also, find out what adaptations professional moderators make in their own performances from one research study to another.

4. Obtain a transcript from a focus group interview. (You may record and transcribe your own mock focus group if necessary.) Point out where (and how) the moderator verbally (and nonverbally if video is available) shifted the group discussion to another topic, stopped a particular participant from responding, encouraged another to respond, and so on.

DATA ANALYSIS

OVERVIEW

Data analysis of focus group data is the aspect of applying focus groups for research purposes that gives most researchers the greatest concern. It is not uncommon for a single focus group transcript to be 50 to 70 pages in length, not including notes from the moderator. If more than one focus group is conducted, as is frequently the case, the amount of data that needs to be transcribed, organized, and reduced to cogent findings quickly becomes overwhelming.

Much of the research conducted in education and psychology follows deductive models. Recently, there have been persuasive arguments for the use and application of inductive approaches to generating concepts and hypotheses in both education and psychology. The data that result from focus group interviews lend themselves to this inductive, qualitative approach. Our suggestion, as well as that of other researchers (e.g., Morgan, 1988), is that if you feel uncomfortable with qualitative findings and your sole intention is to convert them to quantitative data, your research would benefit from a methodology more appropriate for quantitative analysis (e.g., the development and implementation of a survey). If, however, you are interested in the language of the participants and are willing to work with the data to identify units of information that contribute to themes or findings, the application of qualitative data analyses from focus groups can be an informative methodology. This does not mean that focus group data cannot be quantified. In fact, the procedures we describe provide a means for the quantification of the data.

CHAPTER 7

◆ Procedures for a thorough description of the subjects for the focus group studies are described and noted to be similar to those in quantitative methodology.

◆ Recommendations for activities that should be undertaken prior to data analysis are discussed. They include notes and member checks during the interview, procedures for data transcription, and summarization of key ideas.

◆ A step-by-step method of data analysis is recommended. Steps include identifying the big ideas, unitizing the data, categorizing the units, negotiating categories, and identifying themes and using theory.

Qualitative Data Analysis

Although information exists on how and why to use qualitative research methodologies, there is considerably less information on the "nuts and bolts" of what to do with the data after the research has been conducted. Many researchers feel overwhelmed by the volume of transcripts yielded from focus groups and are unsure of how to summarize or reduce the data. There are a number of resources available to researchers that provide excellent overviews of the application of and rationales for qualitative methodology (Bogdan & Biklen, 1992; Glesne & Peshkin, 1992; Patton, 1990). Other resources exist that provide explanations for the types of reliability and validity available through qualitative research (e.g., Maxwell, 1992; Yin, 1989).

In the next section of this chapter, we identify researchers' greatest fears about data analysis procedures for focus group data and provide some suggestions for how to adequately address these concerns. Perhaps the most difficult thing to conceptualize is *how* the narrative information obtained can be *summarized* accurately and, in particular, reliably. Furthermore, without having done it before, *how* does one get started? What does one do first and who should do it? How long can one expect the data analysis procedures to take? How much confidence can one have in the findings when finished? These are commonly expressed questions, and it is our intention in the following step-by-step process to address these fundamental questions as well as others that relate to analysis of focus group data.

DID YOU KNOW THAT?

Focus groups can yield data that are highly consistent with survey data. In an item-by-item analysis of a quantitative survey on food shopping and food preparation compared with findings on the same topic from a series of focus groups, Reynolds and Johnson (1978) revealed that there was a 97% correspondence in findings. The only item in which there were discernible differences was "baking," and later sales figures revealed that the findings from the focus group were the better predictor of consumers' responses.

Description of Subjects
and Group

In many ways, interpreting and summarizing focus group findings is similar to the methodology used in most quantitative studies. As with quantitative methodologies, a thorough and adequate
description of the subject selection procedures and participants
must be provided. This includes the criteria established for purposive sampling, how subjects were identified, how subjects were
contacted, the number of subjects contacted, the percentage of those
subjects who agreed to participate, and the percentage who eventually participated. After reviewing more than 150 articles that have
used focus group methodology, it is our observation that this aspect
of focus group reporting is frequently neglected. Often, only the
number of subjects is reported. Occasionally, descriptive information is mentioned about the subjects who participated (e.g., sex, age
range, income level). Rarely, however, are the procedures for subject
selection, frequency of subjects recruited who participated, or other
relevant information about the subjects or group included in the
write-up. A thorough description of the subjects in the group is
necessary as is a description of incentives provided and the extent
to which researchers demonstrated appropriate efforts to obtain the
participation of designated subjects. By keeping accurate notes and
following the procedures for subject selection and recruitment
advocated earlier in this book, a thorough subject description is
possible, which will clearly aid others in the interpretation of the
findings. (An example of a subject description based on multiple
focus group interviews is provided in Table 7.1.)

Considerations Prior
to Data Analysis

Prior to data analysis, there are several things that a researcher
can do to make the data analysis less difficult. These include taking
notes during the interview, making member checks during the
interview, applying appropriate procedures for transcribing the data,
and summarizing big ideas from the focus group interview imme-

TABLE 7.1 An Example of Subject Description Based on Multiple Focus Group Interviews

Category	Chapter 1	Elementary Special Ed.	Gifted	Regular	Middle Regular	Special Ed.	Gifted	High Regular	Special Ed.	Gifted
Gender										
Male	0	1	0	1	3	2	2	3	1	1
Female	7	3	5	8	9	9	4	1	10	3
Unreported	1	0	0	0	0	0	0	0	0	0
Highest Degree Held										
Bachelor's	5	0	1	3	1	6	1	1	6	2
Master's	2	3	4	6	10	3	4	2	2	1
Specialist	1	1	0	0	0	1	0	1	1	0
Doctor	0	0	0	0	1	0	1	0	0	1
Unreported	0	0	0	0	0	1	0	0	2	0
Ethnicity										
Black/Person of color	2	0	0	1	3	1	0	0	0	0
Caucasian/Non-Hispanic	2	4	4	4	5	4	3	2	6	2
Caucasian/Hispanic	3	0	1	4	3	5	3	2	4	2
Other	0	0	0	0	1	1	0	0	0	0
Unreported	1	0	0	0	0	0	0	0	1	0
Years of Teaching Experience										
1 to 5	3	0	1	1	0	4	0	0	1	1
6 to 10	0	0	1	7	4	2	2	1	4	0
11 to 15	3	0	0	1	5	3	1	0	2	1
16 to 20	1	1	1	0	2	2	0	3	2	1
21+	0	3	2	0	1	0	3	0	0	1
Unreported	1	0	0	0	0	0	0	0	1	0
None (training)	0	0	0	0	0	0	0	0	1	0

SOURCE: Vaughn, Schumm, Jallad, et al. (in press).

diately on its completion. Further descriptions of these procedures follow.

Notes and Member Checks During the Interview. While the focus group is being conducted, one should keep extensive notes on the nonverbal and verbal responses of participants to the key issues. This information will help with the interpretation of the transcripts (Brodigan, 1992; Karger, 1987). Furthermore, if a participant makes a statement with an emotional message (e.g., sarcasm or anger), it is important that this be noted during the interview to assist in the interpretation of the findings.

It is possible while conducting the focus group interview to introduce procedures that will later assist with data analysis. For example, the moderator can use flip charts to identify key ideas that the participants have generated and then attempt to get a feeling from group members as to the extent they support or do not support these ideas.

Basch (1987) indicates that data from focus group interviews are not designed to reflect the strength of people's feelings or convictions. There are, however, procedures for identifying the strength of individual's feelings, and these can be used. For example, the moderator can identify an opinion and then ask the participants to indicate on a 1 to 5 scale how strongly they agree or disagree with the opinion. This information can be supplied either publicly or confidentially to the moderator.

Procedures for Data Transcription. The transcription of the focus groups should be considered prior to their conduct and analysis. Because data analysis should be initiated as soon after the conduct of the focus groups as possible, focus groups should be transcribed immediately after they are conducted. There are several issues regarding transcriptions that need to be determined by the researcher. The first issue is *who should transcribe* the focus group. The answer to this question depends on the resources available to the researcher as well as the purpose of the research. If adequate resources are available, the focus group can be transcribed by a secretary and then examined carefully by the moderator (or other researchers who attended the focus group) to determine accuracy. If secretarial services are not available, then the transcription is best done by the researcher who attended the focus group and who, ideally, will also be the person responsible for the data analysis.

Another issue related to transcription is *how much detail* should be included when the focus group is transcribed. Is it necessary to transcribe every word of every participant? If participants are talking about unrelated topics, should this be transcribed? It is our experience that the easiest data analysis procedure occurs with the most accurate and complete transcript. Even unrelated information is relevant to the data analysis because it provides evidence of the amount of time spent on and off the topic. Also, it is possible that one of the questions related to the focus group was particularly difficult for the participants to address, and, consequently, extensive off-topic time occurred during this question but not during other questions. This information assists in the interpretation of the findings and provides an understanding of the effectiveness of the focus group.

Who should conduct the analyses? Ideally, the investigator should attend the focus group and take the lead in analyzing the data. This may not be realistic when multiple focus groups are conducted. In such cases, the investigator should appoint a capable, well-trained researcher to take the lead in data analysis.

In summary, prior to data analysis, the primary researcher responsible for analyses should attend the focus group, take notes on verbal and nonverbal messages that are relevant to the findings but unlikely to appear in the transcripts, view the videotape or listen to the audiotape another time, read the transcripts from the focus group and ensure that they are accurate, and obtain confirmation from the moderator on the interpretation of selected participants' comments when the intention may be somewhat ambiguous.

Summarize Key Ideas. It is useful to summarize key ideas immediately following the focus group, both to help organize the experience for the moderator and to provide some central ideas for data analysis (Brodigan, 1992). This does not suggest that conclusions are drawn prior to analyzing the data. Rather, this process is intended to provide initial reactions to participants' comments.

We agree with Krueger (1988) that it is essential to consider the following approaches:

1. *Find the big ideas.* These big ideas emerge from multiple data sources, including body language, the words of the participants, the emotional level associated with responses, intensity of comments, and consistent convergence from several participants (not necessarily all) on a particular issue. This requires that the researcher look for patterns of findings rather than counting the number of times something is said. Egbert (1983) reminds us that focus group interviews are qualitative research and that they are best considered as idea generative rather than as an alternative source of quantitative data.

2. *Consider the choice and meaning of words.* When interpreting the findings, consider what words the participants choose to address the issues as well as the meanings intended by the participants. If the meaning is unclear, the interviewer can probe to obtain further information.

3. *Consider the context.* To what extent does it appear that participants' comments were influenced by what others said or by the situation in which the focus group occurred? Would these same responses have occurred if the participants were personally interviewed?

4. *Consider the consistency of responses.* To what extent are the participants' responses consistent throughout the interview? Do the participants change their positions? Under what conditions? Was there a stimulus that occurred prior to a shift in the positions of several participants?

Methods of Analysis

Because there are many uses of focus group interviews, there are also many ways in which the data can be analyzed (Bers, 1987). Some researchers identify themes, post them on charts in prominent places on the wall where they are working, and then provide supporting evidence for these themes from participants' quotes or researchers' notes. Other researchers who are interested in the themes from the focus groups in only the broadest sense, read through the transcripts searching for big ideas and then confirm these ideas through a check with another researcher. With few exceptions, there has been surprisingly little attention to the analysis procedures and the validity of these procedures when applied to focus group interviews (Nelson & Frontczak, 1988). Data analysis descriptions for focus group interviews are notoriously brief and

provide little information about how the data were actually analyzed. Most of the emphasis has been placed on the data collection
procedures. Bertrand, Brown, and Ward (1992) observed the following:

> There is minimal explanation of just what the analyst does and
> writes down. . . . It is unclear why so little has been written on the
> mechanics of the final steps of the research. Perhaps some consider
> that the procedure is self-evident and worthy of only the briefest
> mention. Others may feel that the techniques are not scientific
> enough to merit elaboration. A third reason may be that given the
> degree of insight and intuition necessary to the analysis of qualita-
> tive data, the question of how to approach the data is seen as the
> prerogative of the researcher. Finally, some writers may feel that
> because focus groups are often used as a quick method to get
> suggestive data for program planning purposes, it is not necessary
> to require a systematic approach to data analysis. (p. 200)

Following is the step-by-step procedure that we use when
analyzing data from focus groups. We realize that there are different
effective procedures used by other investigators, but it is often helpful
to know precisely how someone else's data analysis procedures are
implemented so that these same steps can either be followed by or
modified to suit the specific researcher. The procedures that we use
are an adaptation of the Constant Comparative Method (Glaser &
Strauss, 1967) and naturalistic inquiry (Lincoln & Guba, 1985).

SUMMING UP . . .

Lederman (1990) identified analytic approaches that could
be used for data analysis. These include the following:

1. Code data into predetermined categories.
2. Develop categories based on the data and then code the data.
3. Use the data as a basis for summary statements that capture
   the main ideas of the interviewer.
4. Interpret the data through an intensive analytic technique.

We suggest that, when applying any of these procedures,
one should use quotes from the participants to support the
categories, main ideas, and summary statements.

Step 1: Identifying the Big Ideas

Much of Step 1 actually occurs during and immediately follow-ing the focus group interview. The researcher considers the partici-pants' words, ideas that occupied the focus group, intensity of participants' responses, as well as nonverbal communication, and identifies several *big ideas* that represent the findings from the focus group. These big ideas will likely be altered or refined after further data analysis. Nonetheless, they provide the initial framework for the development of the major findings. We feel that this step is important because much of what occurs in later steps requires *unitizing* the data. Such unitization may require the researcher to think about smaller bits of data, and thus the researcher could subsequently "miss the forest for the trees."

Folch-Lyon and Trost (1981) refer to the process as requiring careful digesting of all the key ideas and distinguishing the strong, significant themes from the less significant ones. This is a fairly sophisticated process because it requires more than just counting how often an idea is reported. It requires an awareness of the extent to which the theme is an emotional one or is important for a few of the participants versus all of the participants. At this stage, the big ideas or themes are identified as impressions or hypotheses rather than as definite findings. According to Krueger (1988), "the analysis process is like detective work. One looks for clues, but in this case, the clues are trends and patterns that reappear among various focus groups" (p. 109). Thus, the big ideas are ones that emerge after involvement, rereading, and careful consideration of data in the focus groups. Even so, considerable subjective judgment is involved in the selection and interpretation. This step is revisited at the end of the unit analyses.

Step 2: Unitizing the Data

This refers to the process of identifying those units of informa-tion that will later become the basis for defining categories. There are several important things to consider when identifying units:

1. For a piece of information to be a unit, it should be *heuristic* or aimed at assisting the researcher to better understand the topic or

research question. If the information does not meet the criteria of better informing the research question, it is not relevant—even if it is interesting.

2. A unit should be the smallest amount of information that is informative by itself. This unit of information should be interpretable without more than a broad understanding of the purpose of the study.

3. The size of a unit of information can vary from a phrase to a sentence or a paragraph.

4. Whenever possible, the unit of information should include a direct quote from a participant in the focus group.

We have found that experience coding interviews facilitates the process considerably. Initially, unit identification is a very time-consuming process. The experienced qualitative data analyst, however, is able to move rapidly through this step of the process.

What are some of the considerations when identifying units? As with all aspects of the focus group interview, it is essential that the data analyst be very familiar with the purpose of the research and the research questions. One should make several copies of the transcript from the focus group interview and then read through one copy of the transcript to identify relevant information.

We identify relevant information through one of two procedures. One procedure is using a highlighter to mark the information units and another is typing the units into the computer. The latter procedure is more time-consuming and requires retyping much of the data that has already been transcribed. For the first-time analyst, however, the entering of information into the computer is often a necessary step. If the computer process is used, it is essential that a data log be established identifying the data source, subject, and where the data information can be found. This simplifies things later when someone needs to verify information by locating it in the original transcript.

SUMMING UP . . .

Bertrand, Brown, et al. (1992) use an approach referred to as *margin coding*. Themes are identified, and then numbers and letters are used to represent the themes. The analyst reads through the transcript and writes the appropriate thematic code next to comments that relate to each of the themes. This approach is useful when only a quick survey of the main ideas is required and extensive data analysis procedures are not needed to meet the goals of the study.

Whether the units are identified through highlighting or through entry into the computer, the next step is to cut the information units into separate slips of paper so that they can be categorized. Once the units are highlighted, the relevant subject and transcript location information needs to be provided through a code on each of the information units. This process will have already been taken care of if the information units were entered into the computer. Next, all the relevant information units—and the information codes that provide relevant information about them—are separated from the text. At this point, categorizing the units is possible.

Step 3: Categorizing the Units

In this step, the units that were identified in Step 2 are sorted into relevant *piles* that will eventually represent categories or themes. Categorizing brings together those information units that are related to the same content. Categories are superordinate headings that provide an organizational *theme* for the units of data.

During this step, rules that describe category properties are defined to justify the inclusion of units into that category and also to serve as a basis for later tests of intersorter reliability. Adequate time should be allotted to complete this procedure. Many people find it disconcerting to be interrupted while categorizing the units and need extensive time free from interruption. These are the procedures to follow for categorizing units:

1. The initial categories will emerge from the information available after participating in the focus group, reading the transcript, and identifying the units of information. Briefly describe the criteria for each category on a separate sheet of paper and place it next to a large manila envelope with the name of the category on the outside of the envelope. Look through information units that contribute directly to that category or would be sorted as representing that category. Put these information units into the envelope. As you work with information units, you may need to revise the criteria for the category. When you have identified all information units that directly relate to the category, carefully review them and look for any examples that do not relate. Consider your criteria for inclusion into the category and determine the extent to which the criteria are accurate and reflect all information units for that category.

2. Continue this process with other categories until you have exhausted those categories that are most apparent. It is likely that while engaged in the process you will think of other categories. Jot down these category titles and initial criteria, and you can return to them after you finish the one that you are working on. Categories emerge rapidly at first but more slowly as you progress with the sorting.

3. After you have continued with this process for a while, you will find information units that do not fit with established categories and yet do not seem to warrant their own category either. Simply place these information units in a miscellaneous pile that you will return to later.

4. Identifying rules or criteria for a category is an ongoing process that occurs while you are developing the category and then again after all of the information units have been placed in the category. Particularly when there are a considerable number of information units in a category (e.g., more than six), the rules for placement of information in the category need to be reconsidered and rewritten to ensure that all information units relate. If not, information units may need to be withdrawn from that category.

5. Once all of the information units have been exhausted, review the categories for overlap and completeness. Sometimes categories have similar properties. These can be collapsed into a broader category that includes all of the information in the previously separate categories. When this occurs, the rules or criteria for inclusion of

information units into the categories need to be reconsidered. It is also possible that a category has been created that is too large and should be subdivided into more than one category.

6. What do you do with the information units still remaining in the miscellaneous pile? First, reread and reconsider them in light of the newly revised categories. If any can be appropriately placed in the new categories, do so. Second, consider whether any of the information units should not have been included and actually do not provide relevant information that leads to a better understanding of the research question. Because data analysts should err in the direction of overincluding information units, it is possible that some are not relevant and should be discarded. Third, some information units provide relevant information that contributes to the understanding of the study but does not fit with any of the existing categories. These information units become categories of their own. At this point, all miscellaneous slips should be dealt with and either included in other categories, used as their own category, or discarded.

Step 4: Negotiating Categories

Steps 1 through 3 should be completed by a data analyst working alone. After two data analysts have each completed these steps alone, the next step is for them to work together to negotiate and compare their categories. Again, our experience is that this requires considerable time and effort and that it should be conducted in a quiet room with few distractions or interruptions. We also have observed that, although many people can be taught to analyze data according to the previously identified steps, there are people who have considerable difficulty with negotiating their categories. They have put considerable effort into the development of their category names and the criteria for inclusion of information units and are resistant to working cooperatively with another data analyst to consider the possibility that another category name, criterion, or different category altogether might be superior. Our experience is that it is not hard to identify people who will have extreme difficulty with this step and therefore should not be included in the data analysis process.

The procedures we recommend for this step in the process are the following:

1. The two data analysts meet in a quiet room free from distractions with their categorized data, including manila envelopes representing each category with the title of the category, rules and criteria for inclusion of units in each category, and units of information within the envelope for each category.

2. One of the data analysts selects a category considered to be highly representative of the data (a category that was easily formed), reads the title and the rules or criteria for the category, and asks whether the other data analyst has a similar category.

3. If the other data analyst has a similar category, its title and corresponding rules or criteria should also be read aloud. Then the two data analysts discuss the similarities and differences of their categories, reconstruct the criteria or rules so that they apply to both, devise a new title (or use one of the two suggested), and determine the extent to which all of the information units within the category have been consistently categorized. Information units that do not fit are set aside, and information units from other categories that are appropriate are included. When both data analysts agree that the category title, rules or criteria for inclusion of information units, and the information units included in the category are correct, they move on to the next category.

4. The process continues until the data analysts have exhausted all of their categories. As long as there is agreement between the data analysts about category titles, rules, and information units, the process proceeds rather smoothly—albeit with lengthy discussions about the appropriate choices of words for titles and the use of particular information sources within a specific category. Often the meaning of the titles are the same even though the word choice may be different. In these cases, resolving differences is relatively easy.

5. What should be done when disagreement between the data analysts cannot be resolved through discussion and adjustments to the category titles and rules? If this problem occurs with most of the categories in the data set, then one or more problems have likely occurred. First, determine whether one or both data analysts have competently categorized their data. If one person has not done a particularly thorough job, it is possible that this is affecting the agreement of categories between the analysts. Second, determine if one or both data analysts are stubbornly clinging to their categories and are unwilling to make minor adjustments that would facilitate category agreement. Third, determine whether the categories selected by one or both data analysts are appropriate and relevant to the research questions. If the problem is not a pervasive one but merely a difficulty with one or more categories, then the involve-

TABLE 7.2 Pointers for Analyzing Focus Group Interview Data

- Initiate data analysis as soon as possible after the focus group is conducted.
- Assess the amount of time the participants spent on each issue. To some extent, this may have been affected by the moderator, who determined how long each question was discussed.
- Determine how much probing and guiding the moderator did versus how much of the discussion naturally flowed from the participants.
- Identify the intensity of people's reactions to issues and the extent to which people feel strongly or emotionally involved in the issues. An important next step is to examine the data for the reasons and rationales people provided for why they feel the way they do.
- Identify those participant responses that appear as though the intention was to please the moderator (or other members of the group) rather than to provide the honest, genuine feedback.
- Look for future tense, conditional, and third-party statements versus present tense, unconditional, "I" statements.
- Be aware that there is often a dominator in the group and try to tune out his or her effect when analyzing the results.
- Look for majority and minority opinions. Recognize that consensus need not occur.
- Look for consistencies and inconsistencies in people's responses and in their reactions to the responses of others.

ment of one or more experienced data analysts to read and provide an independent interpretation to resolve the conflict is sufficient.

A summary of pointers for analyzing focus group interview data is provided in Table 7.2.

What does the researcher do when more than one focus group has been conducted? First, it is helpful if the same data analysts have attended all of the focus groups and therefore can complete data analysis on all of the focus groups. Second, the same procedures identified above for a single focus group are completed separately for each of the additional focus groups. Once the themes, categories, and supporting evidence have been decided for each individual focus group, then all of the data analysts meet to code data across focus groups. Their goal is to identify common themes and categories across focus groups. The number of focus groups that support those themes and categories are noted. This process continues until all themes and categories have been accounted for. Thus, if six separate focus groups have been conducted, when cross-focus-group analysis occurs, it is possible to have themes that are supported by as many as six of the focus groups and as few as one.

Step 5: Identifying Themes and Use of Theory

The first step in the data analysis process was to consider the big ideas. Essentially, Step 5 reexamines the ideas generated in the first step. Consider if any of the big ideas established in the first step are supported by the categories generated. In light of the work done with the information units and categories, how should those big ideas be reframed and restated? We refer to these refined ideas as *themes*. The themes consider the big ideas from the focus group data as well as the information units and categories. The researcher's role is to identify the themes and determine the extent to which categories support these themes.

SUMMING UP . . .

Another way to sort information units is by using index cards. Lewis, Kitano, and Lynch (1992) conducted a study of the affective characteristics of academically gifted adults through the use of focus groups. They used the following steps:

1. Participant responses were written on 3" x 5" index cards.
2. Cards were kept in order from the first comment made by a participant to the last.
3. Index cards were color coded by session and included the number from the session.
4. Researchers used two theories that had formed the framework for the study to categorize and interpret the data.
5. Two independent researchers developed categories that were reviewed by the three-member research team.

Theory plays an important role in data analysis, but how and when it is used depends on the purpose of the study, the research questions, and the extent to which theory has influenced the development of the research to that point. Because focus groups are often used when little information is available on a topic, it is possible that the study may have few predetermined theoretical underpinnings. As Yin (1989) advised, the theoretical propositions that led to the study should be identified early on and used as a framework for developing data analysis. For example, in a study we conducted to investigate general education teacher planning for students with disabilities, we used a model of teacher planning. The elements of this model guided the way in which we selected the categories to report our data. The steps provided for data analysis in this section do not provide a specific role for theory until after all of the data analyses are conducted. Then, theory is considered to assist in interpreting the categories and findings.

DID YOU KNOW THAT?

The quality of the ideas from a focus group interview can be rated on a 1 to 5 scale by two independent raters. Using two graduate students in this way, Nelson and Frontczak (1988) found relatively good reliability between raters ranging from 0.76 for quantity of responses to 0.59 for quality of responses. Considering that they were rated on a five-point scale, 0.59 is relatively high interrater reliability.

Use of Computers for Data Analysis

There are essentially two ways computers can assist with analysis of data from focus group interviews. First, word processing is a necessary step in the transcription and revision of focus group data. Second, computers can assist with the mechanical duties of organizing data and identifying themes. As indicated in the previous description of the step-by-step process recommended for the analysis of qualitative data, much of the data organization involves cutting and pasting, which is cumbersome work. Computer programs can reduce this process and assist with the organizational steps. We feel, however, that a warning is necessary. Computer programs are a tool that may be useful in assembling and locating information, but computers have yet to provide assistance in the interpretation of findings and the identification of significant themes (other than those most frequently identified). Furthermore, they cannot interpret the emotional tone, which is so critical to understanding the findings from many focus group interviews. Table 7.3 provides an overview of the most popular qualitative data analysis software packages available, and Table 7.4 lists the distributors of these software packages. For a more thorough review of the use and application of computer programs in qualitative data analysis, see Miles and Huberman (1994).

ACTIVITIES

1. Conduct a mock focus group with a few friends in which you audiotape their responses to preidentified questions. Transcribe the tape. Use the transcript to see if you can identify *units of information.* Ask one of your friends who attended the focus group to do the same thing. How close were you in identifying the same units of information?

2. Use the units of information identified in Activity 1 and categorize them. Ask your friend to do the same thing. Be sure to identify the rules or criteria for inclusion in the categories. Meet with your friend and determine the extent to which you identified similar and dissimilar categories. Negotiate differences.

3. Identify the procedure that you could use if you were unable to resolve differences when negotiating categories with another researcher. What are some of the potential explanations for why this occurred?

4. Read the sections from the Lincoln and Guba (1985) book, *Naturalistic Inquiry,* that address reliability and validity. What is their approach to validity and reliability, and how does it compare with descriptions from a more quantitative model?

TABLE 7.3. Software Program Characteristics

	Version	Operating System	Coding	Search & Retrieval	Database Mgmt	Memoing	Data linking	Matrix building	Network display	Theory-building	User friendliness
AQUAD	[3.2]	D	■	◐	□	■		◐		■	✓✓
askSam	[5.1]	DW		●	■	□	■		■		✓✓
ATLAS/ti	[1.0e]	D	■	◐	□	■	■	○	●a	■	✓✓✓
Folio Views	[3.0]	DW	■	●	■	■	■	○			✓✓✓
HyperQual b	[4.3]	Mc	■	○	■	■	■	○			✓✓
HyperRESEARCH	[1.5]	McW	■	◐	□			○		■	✓✓✓
Inspiration	[4.0]	Mc		○		■	■		●		✓✓✓
Kwalitan	[3.1]	D	■	◐	□	■	□	■		□	✓✓✓
MAX b	[3.x]	D	■	○	■		■				✓✓
MECA	[1.0]	McDU				■		◐	■		✓✓
Meta Design	[4.0]	McW		○		□	■		●		✓✓
Metamorph c	[3.5]	McDUM		●d	□	□	■				✓
	[4.0]	McWU	□	●d	□	■	■				✓✓
NUDIST	[2.3]	McWUM	■	●	□		□	◐		■	✓
	[3.0]	Mc	■	●	□	■	□	●	◐	■	✓✓
Orbis b,e	[1.0]	DW	□	●	■	□	□	●			✓✓
QCA	[3.0]	D		○		□		◐		■	✓
QUALPRO	[4.0]	D	■	◐	□	□					✓✓✓
SemNet	[1.0.2]	Mc		◐		■	■		●	■	✓✓
Sonar Professional	[8.4]	McW		●	□	■	■	□		□	✓✓
The Ethnograph	[4.0]	D	■	◐	□	■		○			✓✓
The Text Collector	[1.7]	D		●	□						✓✓✓
WordCruncher	[4.5]	D		◐	□		■				✓
	[Beta]	W		●	□	■	■				✓✓
ZyIndex	[5.0]	DW		●	□	■	■				✓

■	=	Designed for this purpose, as we see it (May be more or less effective)
□	=	Not really designed for it, but can do at least in a limited way
blank	=	Can't do this

●	=	Strong	✓	=	Not too friendly
◐	=	OK	✓✓	=	Fairly friendly
○	=	Weak	✓✓✓	=	Very friendly
blank	=	absent			

Operating System: Mc = Macintosh;   D = DOS;   U = Unix;
                      M = Main Frame;   W = Windows

SOURCE: M. B. Miles and A. M. Huberman, *An Expanded Sourcebook: Qualititative Data Analysis* (2nd ed.), p. 316. Copyright 1994 by authors. Reprinted by permission of Sage Publications, Inc.

a. Weaker than Inspiration and MetaDesign on graphics, but can create networks from data.

b. Reviewed from documentation, so ratings are somewhat speculative.

c. Based on version 3.5 and a demo of version 4.0, so ratings for 4.0 are somewhat speculative.

d. For raw text retrieval, in a class by itself.

e. Available as add-on module for XyWrite 4.0 or NotaBene 4.0 word processors. Ratings include word processor features.

TABLE 7.4 Names, Addresses, and Numbers for the Software
Distributors From Table 7.3

AQUAD, ATLAS/ti, HyperQual, MAX, QUALPRO, and The Ethnograph are all available from:	Qualitative Research Management 73425 Hilltop Road Desert Springs, CA 92241 Tel. (619) 329-7026 Fax. (619) 329-0223
askSam is available from:	askSam Systems P.O. Box 1428 119 S. Washington Street Perry, FL 32347 Tel. 1-800-800-1997 Fax. (904) 584-7481
Folio Views is available from:	Folio Corporation 5072 N. 300 West Provo, UT 84604 Tel. 1-800-543-6346 Fax. (801) 229-6790
HyperRESEARCH is available from:	Researchware, Inc. 20 Soren Street Randloph, MA 02368-1945 Tel. (617) 961-3909
Inspiration is available from:	Inspiration Software, Inc. 7412 SW Beaverton Hillsdale Highway, Suite 102 Portland, OR 97225 Tel. (503) 297-3004 Fax. (503) 297-4676
Kwalitan is available from:	Vincent Peters, Department of Research Methodology Social Sciences Faculty, University of Nijmegen Th. van Acquinostraat 4 6525 GD Nijmegen, The Netherlands Tel. 31-80-612038 Fax. 31-80-612351 E-mail: U211384@HNYKUN11
MECA is available from:	Kathleen Carley, Dept. of Social and Decision Sciences, Carnegie Mellon University, Pittsburgh, PA 15568 Tel. (412) 268-3225 E-mail: Kathleen.Carley%CENTRO. SOAR.CS.CMU.EDU@Carnegie.bitnet
Meta Design is available from:	Meta Software Corporation 125 Cambridge Park Drive Cambridge, MA 02140 Tel. (617) 576-6920 Fax. (617) 661-2008

TABLE 7.4 Continued

Metamorph is available from:	Thunderstone Expansion Programs International, Inc. 11115 Edgewater Drive Cleveland, OH 44102 Tel. (216) 631-8544 Fax. (216) 281-0828
NUDIST is available from:	Qualitative Solutions and Research Pty Ltd., 2 Research Drive La Trobe University Melbourne, Vic. 3083 Australia Tel. 61-3-479-1311 Fax. 61-3-479-4441 E-mail: nudist@latcs1.lat.oz.au
Orbis is available from:	XYQuest, The Technology Group 36 S. Charles Street Baltimore, MD 21201 Tel. (410) 576-2040 Fax. (410) 576-1968
QCA is available from:	Center for Urban Affairs and Policy Research Northwestern University Evanston, IL 60208 Tel. (708) 491-8712 E-mail: kadrass@nevada. edu; cragin@nwu.edu
SemNet is available from:	Dr. Joseph Faletti 1043 University Avenue San Diego, CA 92103 Tel. (619) 594-5200
Sonar Professional is available from:	Virginia Systems, Inc. 5509 West Bay Court Midlothian, VA 23112 Tel. (804) 739-3200
The Text Collector is available from:	O'Neill Software P.O. Box 26111 San Francisco, CA 94126 Tel. Fax. (415) 398-2255
WordCruncher is available from:	Johnston & Co. 314 E. Carlyle Ave. Alpine, UT 84004 Tel. (812) 339-9996
ZyIndex is available from:	ZyLAB Corporation 100 Lexington Drive Buffalo Grove, IL 60089 Tel. 1-800-544-6339 Fax. (708) 459-8054

PUTTING IT ALL TOGETHER

Steps in Conducting
Focus Group Interviews

OVERVIEW

This chapter describes, in a step-by-step format, the sequence of actions necessary to develop, implement, and interpret successful focus group interviews. Each step will in part be a summary of the main points expounded in other chapters. The reader is frequently asked to return to specific chapters for more detailed descriptions and explanations of particular components of focus group interviews.

CHAPTER 8

KEY IDEAS IN THIS CHAPTER

◆ There exists a clear methodology for the development, use, and analysis of focus group interviews.

◆ Each step is built on the previous steps.

◆ Due care given to earlier steps will enhance the ease with which later steps are completed.

Step 1: Delineate the General Purpose

A clear understanding of the research aims facilitates the use and application of the focus group interview. Establishing a clear purpose lays the groundwork for the entire research project (e.g., it structures later decisions regarding sampling and number of focus groups). It is recommended that a general purpose statement be drafted and agreed on by all those with a vested interest in the research project. (A sample general purpose statement and more detailed discussion of the general purpose statement are presented in Chapter 4.) This statement should include the research topic and general project objectives.

Given the suggested period of time for a focus group interview (approximately 90 minutes) and the recommended number of participants (between 8 and 10), the number of research objectives should optimally be limited to two or three. Otherwise, insufficient time will be available for each interested participant to respond adequately to all of the objectives.

Step 2: Designate a Moderator

The moderator is the key to a successful focus group interview. The moderator promotes the interaction of the participants and ensures that the focus group discussion does not digress from the stated topic. In so doing, the moderator maintains a supportive and nonevaluative environment while controlling any participants who become disruptive. In addition, the moderator is often involved in the focus group preparations and in the analyses of the data.

Moderators may be members of the research team or outside professionals hired for the sole purpose of moderating the focus group interviews. In either situation, the moderator must possess effective interviewing skills, group processing skills, and a thorough knowledge of the research objectives.

When selecting a focus group moderator, keep in mind how characteristics of the moderator (e.g., sex, age, race) may influence the participants' responses. (Because the moderator serves such a vital role, Chapter 6 deals exclusively with this topic and covers everything from how to select and train a moderator to the moderator's part in analyzing the focus group interview data.)

Step 3: Refine the Research Goals

After developing the general purpose statement, it is necessary to further refine the area or areas of interest. This is accomplished by constructing lists of specific information that the researchers both *want* and *do not want* to gain from the focus group interviews. This process also helps delineate for the moderator which specific types of information on which specific topics are desired from the participants. Also this list can be used to later extrapolate the focus group questions and probes that will most accurately reflect the aims of the study. (Such lists are illustrated in Chapter 4.)

Next, it is essential to consider how the data from the focus group interviews will be used. Focus group interviews may be a study in and of themselves, or they may be one part of a larger research project. (Examples of many of the specific uses for focus group interviews are listed in Chapter 4.) Once the use of the focus group data has been determined, the criteria for ascertaining the success of the focus group interviews must be established from the list of wanted information. This often includes pre-identifying certain comments and types of information that are likely to be proffered by the participants. (Examples of these are also included in Chapter 4.)

Step 4: Select the Participants

Focus group participants are often selected through purposive sampling. Thus, a list of the types of participants (e.g., psychologists in private practice, elementary school science teachers) who may be needed to address the research issue is developed. This list is then divided into those participants who are necessary and those who would be helpful but are not essential to the focus group interviews.

Researchers are encouraged to develop a screening procedure to aid in the selection of subjects for the focus group interview. The development of a screening procedure will help ensure that the appropriate participants are included in the focus group interviews. The screening procedure should include the specific questions to elicit information from potential participants that will better allow the researcher to determine that the focus group interview includes the participants who will be most effective. The questions contained in the screening procedure should describe the participants in areas relevant to the research project. This information can be used later during the analyses to describe the sample.

When selecting participants and designating them to different focus groups, it is important to consider the implications of homogeneity versus heterogeneity. (Chapter 5 describes the benefits and limitations associated with each.) It is our observation that homogeneous participants make for more successful focus group interviews than do heterogeneous participants.

Another important area of consideration when selecting participants includes whether the participants should be strangers, acquaintances, or friends. It is often suggested that focus group interview participants be strangers because individuals will be more inclined to be truthful and to freely disclose when they are interacting with people they do not know and presumably will not see again. Also important is the degree of familiarity the participants have with the focus group topic. It is possible that participants who are privy to relevant information that other group members do not know could possibly take on a "one-up" position in the focus group, which could adversely affect the participation of the other group members. The range of perceptions of the participants should also be given attention. It has been generally observed that the presence of a variety of perceptions contributes to a more informative (and hence more successful) focus group interview. Other areas of consideration may be more obvious (e.g., race, sex, and age). (The myriad of characteristics to be delineated are presented in Chapter 5.)

Also important is the amount of information to be given to the participants in preparation for the focus group interviews. This can be problematic because the participants will certainly want to know what will be expected of them, but, if they know too much about the topic prior to the actual focus group interview, they may attempt to alter their responses (e.g., changing them in socially desirable ways, finding out more about the topic so their responses no longer reflect their natural life experiences). (Recommendations for informing potential participants about their roles in a focus group interview and a sample dialogue are presented in Chapter 5. Also presented in Chapter 5 are suggestions for recruiting participants.)

It has been our experience that people are highly willing to participate in focus group interviews and that they enjoy them when they do participate. The opportunity to be asked their opinions, to be listened to genuinely, and to know that their opinions are anonymous and that their input will influence a decision or a goal are valuable experiences for people. We have found that very few people refuse to participate.

Step 5: Determine the Number of Focus Group Interviews

The number of focus group interviews will, in part, be dependent on the number of different participants (e.g., teachers and principals with each being in a separate focus group) necessary for the success of the focus group interviews. It is recommended that focus group interviews continue to be conducted until the moderator can predict how the participants are going to respond. A single focus group interview is considered inadequate. (The judgments to be made in determining the number of focus group interviews are described in Chapter 4.)

Step 6: Arrange for the Focus Group Facility

When considering a focus group site, it is important to remember the main goal of the facility is to promote the comfort of the participants. (Specific facility requirements, such as accessibility by public transportation, ample parking, and equipment capabilities are discussed in Chapter 4.) It is important to note that the focus group facility should be in a location that is neutral to the participants and that, preferably, is viewed by participants as a retreat.

Professional focus group facilities are available for rent in most larger cities, and universities often have rooms that are adequately equipped. (Chapter 9 describes focus group interview facility considerations with nonadult populations.)

Step 7: Develop an Interview Guide

Develop an interview guideline of the research objectives and ensuing questions that were previously refined in Steps 1 and 3. This guide provides an outline for the focus group interview procedures and a general idea of the questions that will be addressed. The questions developed for focus group interviews should be specific enough to guide the moderator but general enough to leave the interviewer with a great deal of latitude to further probe and elicit information. Also included are possible probes or follow-up remarks to each of the focus group questions. Remember that the interview guide is meant to be just that—a guide—and not a transcript to be rigidly adhered to. (Sample questions and probes are listed in Chapter 6.) It is strongly recommended that the interview guide be pretested in an informal focus group arrangement prior to the conduct of the actual focus group interviews.

Step 8: Conduct the
Focus Group Interview

The moderator (with the assistance of others) prepares the focus group interview facility (e.g., sets up and tests equipment, arranges refreshments) before the participants arrive. Upon their arrival, the moderator passes out paperwork (e.g., consent forms, demographic questionnaires) and name tags, introduces him- or herself to the participants, and introduces the participants to each other. Once this is accomplished, the moderator may begin the focus group interview. The opening statement by the moderator should both put the participants at ease and establish the importance of the task they are about to perform. (Appropriate introductions and opening remarks are demonstrated in Chapter 6. Also in Chapter 6 are further samples of the types of questions, probes, and techniques used by moderators during focus group interviews.)

At the end of the focus group interview, the moderator should invite the participants to report any last comments and thank them again for their participation. This is an effective manner of concluding a focus group interview without prematurely stopping a participant from responding.

Step 9: Analyze the Focus Group Data

Analysis begins by describing the sample. This description should include the size of the group, the individuals who participated and a brief description of their background, the location where the focus group interview took place, and the procedures used for the selection of participants.

Because there are many uses of focus group interviews, there are several methods for analyzing and reporting the findings from focus group interviews. For example, the data can be interpreted in a general way with the moderator reflecting on what would be the major themes, or it can be analyzed in an in-depth way by transcribing the interview tape and coding it according to various methodologies. Most frequently, the focus group interview is transcribed and coded. (This process is illustrated step-by-step in Chapter 7.)

Table 8.1 is a checklist of the steps involved in planning and conducting focus group interviews as well as the steps for analyzing and reporting data generated from focus groups. The table indicates the locations in this book (Chapter/page) where these steps are discussed.

TABLE 8.1 Checklist for Focus Group Interviews

Preparing for the Focus Group Interview
- Identify research problem/purpose (4/38).
- Decide if focus group interviews are compatible with research problem (3/27).
- Write a general purpose statement that reflects your research interest (4/38).
- Refine the purpose statement by developing lists of information that you *do* and *do not* want to obtain from the focus group (4/39).
- Establish goals that relate to how the information gathered from the focus group will be used (4/39).
- Establish goals to identify the outcome required for the focus group to have been successful (4/40).
- Decide on the number of focus groups (4/48).
- Establish the length of time for the focus group (4/50).
- Determine the setting for the focus group (4/51).
- Develop procedures for encouraging attendance (5/65).
- Identify and train a moderator (6/91).
- Prepare the interview guide (4/41).

Selecting Participants
- Develop a sampling plan (5/58).
- Establish criteria for sample selection (5/60).
- Develop and implement screening procedure (5/64).
- Construct a recruitment plan (5/65).
- Invite and orient participants (5/67).

Conducting the Focus Group Interview
- Prepare the room by checking seating arrangements, temperature, and ventilation (6/79).
- Set up refreshments (6/79).
- Set up and check recording equipment (6/79).
- Greet participants and establish welcoming environment (6/77).
- Collect demographic information (6/78).
- Distribute name tags (6/78).
- Orient participants through opening remarks (6/80).
- Initiate focus group discussion (6/78).
- Take notes and conduct member checks during the interview (4/46).

Analyzing and Reporting Data From a Focus Group Interview
- Determine data analysis and reporting plan (7/98).
- Describe subject selection procedures and participants (7/99).
- Transcribe recorded data (7/101).
- Summarize key ideas (7/102).
- Unitize data (7/105).
- Categorize units (7/107).
- Negotiate categories (7/109).
- Identify themes and theory (7/112).
- Draft focus group report (7/103).

USE OF FOCUS GROUPS
WITH CHILDREN AND
ADOLESCENTS

OVERVIEW

As greater importance is placed on obtaining the consumer's point of view and as children and adolescents are becoming more valued as reporters of their own experiences (e.g., Kleiner, 1991), focus group interviews with nonadult populations as the participants are becoming more and more common. As consumers of educational and psychological services, children and adolescents provide unique and valuable perspectives for researchers, clinicians, and educators. Because of their varying developmental levels, when children and adolescents are employed as participants, special considerations and modifications must be made in the focus group interview format. These issues are described below.

CHAPTER 9

KEY IDEAS IN THIS CHAPTER

- ◆ Children and adolescents provide unique and valuable information for researchers interested in their points of view.

- ◆ Child and adolescent focus group participants require more flexibility, direction, and interaction on the part of the moderator than do adult participants.

- ◆ The focus group setting must be arranged to accommodate young participants.

- ◆ The keys to conducting a focus group with children and adolescents are to grab their attention and to keep them active.

Research Issues in Education
and Psychology That Require
Child and Adolescent Subjects

Although teachers' perceptions of instructional practices have been a mainstay of educational research for years, surprisingly little research has addressed students' perceptions. In our work on students' preferences of instructional practices, we have found that the insights of students of all ages can add an interesting dimension to our understanding of what happens in the classroom and how students learn (Vaughn, Schumm, & Kouzekanani, 1993). We have used focus group interviews with students as a baseline for instrument development (Schumm, Vaughn, & Saumell, 1992), to further understand student responses to a survey instrument (Vaughn, Schumm, Niarhos, & Gordon, 1993), and to ascertain students' reactions to instructional interventions (Schumm, Leavell, Gordon, & Murfin, 1993).

In psychology, focus groups can be used for similar purposes. The types of research questions for which child and adolescent participants would be necessary are presented in Table 9.1. Focus

TABLE 9.1 Sample Research Questions for Child and Adolescent
Participants

- What are students' views of teachers' adaptations of instructional materials and methods for special learners?
- What opinions do adolescents hold regarding sex education in school?
- How do students perceive different service delivery models for gifted education?
- How can educational materials about drug abuse be made more attractive to, and effective for, children or adolescents?
- How do youngsters feel toward their mainstreamed classmates?
- In what ways is teasing viewed by adolescents as a positive and negative event, and how does teasing affect them?
- Do male and female adolescents differ in their expectations of dating?
- How do prepubescent children talk about their experiences with classmates diagnosed with eating disorders?

group interviews aid researchers in understanding individuals and families. For example, focus groups with special populations of children or adolescents (e.g., culturally diverse or physically handicapped) can provide valuable information about their unique familial experiences. Focus groups also allow the researcher to gain a more in-depth understanding of the subjects' perceptions, beliefs, attitudes, and experiences. This is particularly relevant when studying children and adolescents, who often use jargon that is specific to their age group and cultural domain. In addition to this increased understanding of the language used by children and adolescents, focus groups clarify children's and adolescents' comprehension of terminology and concepts developed by researchers. Thus they can be used in the development of surveys or rating scales.

SUMMING UP . . .

According to McDonald and Topper (1988), group research with children can be categorized in three ways:

1. The Adult-Oriented approach treats children like small adults and allows for no modifications for the children's developmental levels.

2. The Creative-Drama approach treats children like children and simulates the school environment. The moderator acts as a teacher facilitating game-like activities calling upon the children's creativity.

3. The Structural approach treats children as children but recognizes their different developmental stages and makes accommodations for these differences. The children's ability to speak of their own experiences and to perform structured tasks is more valued than their creativity.

Those methodologies that recognize and make accommodations for children's varying developmental stages are the most effective. The activities to be used (e.g., structured exercises or creative drawing) depend on the research questions.

Age Limits on
Focus Group Participants

With few exceptions, focus groups should not be conducted with children below 6 years of age. Children under the age of 6 years do not have sufficient expressive language to adequately participate in focus group interviews. In addition, until approximately 6 years of age, children's language production (vocabulary) exceeds their comprehension (Schuster & Ashburn, 1992), making the findings from younger children's focus groups difficult to interpret. Thus, the accuracy and legitimacy of their responses may be suspect. Children over 6 years of age, in most cases, are effective focus group participants. In fact, due to their incomplete internalization of socially desirable responses, children are likely to provide more spontaneous responses than some adult participants.

Group Characteristics

The size of the focus group for children and adolescents needs to be smaller (usually around five or six participants) than for adults. Also, the length of the focus group interview should be decreased for children and should be based on the age of the participants. Rather than the 90 minutes allocated for adult focus groups, the focus group should be approximately 45 minutes for children under 10 years and around 60 minutes for children between 10 and 14 years of age.

In addition to changes in the number of participants and length of time of the focus group, the composition of the group also needs to be considered. It is our recommendation and that of other researchers (e.g., Spethmann, 1992) that focus groups with children should be comprised of same-sex participants. Young children and adolescents may be uncomfortable or distracted in a group with individuals of the opposite sex, with the net effect being a greater likelihood of inhibited and externally influenced responses. In addition, the participants should be strangers. If the participants know each other (e.g., are from the same classroom), again the possibility increases of their responses being moderated and thus less than genuine. Another recommendation is that the participants be no more than 2 years apart in age (Spethmann, 1992). If participants are from varying developmental levels, the focus group language and activities will likely bore some of the participants and confuse others. As a result, developmental differences between the participants will make it difficult for the moderator to facilitate the equal involvement of all of the participants.

It is also advantageous to consider whether unique characteristics of particular participants will impede the success of the focus group. For example, a child with attention deficit disorder (i.e., hyperactivity, impulsivity, or attention problems) may manipulate the group discussion and distract or inhibit the responses of the other participants. Other potentially disruptive characteristics to consider include crying, speech difficulties, and behavior problems. During the process of participant selection, it is beneficial to ask parents or guardians, teachers, and other relevant individuals about the child's ability to participate with others in a focus group format. If a child becomes disruptive in the focus group, similar techniques to those recommended in Chapter 7 for disruptive adults may be used to regain control of the group and to promote the participation of all of the participants.

Facility Considerations When Working With Children and Adolescents

It is important that the moderator check the room for appropriateness of size before deciding on a focus group site. A focus group room that is too large may be interpreted as overpowering, especially from the perspective of children. A room that is too small may inhibit the movement of the participants and appear stifling. Also, the furniture arrangement within the room may have an impact on the focus group. If young children are participating, it may be beneficial to be able to sit in a circle on the floor. If exercises are planned (e.g., role playing or drawing), then sufficient open space within the room will be necessary. Furniture that is easily moved will allow for spontaneous or unexpected changes in activities.

The moderator should keep in mind the physical size of the participants. Consider how much fidgeting is going to occur if child participants are expected to sit in chairs made for adults. Furniture that is made in proportion to the participants will work best, and the moderator should use the same furniture as the participants, which literally puts the moderator at the participant's level. As a result, the participants will be less likely to associate the moderator with adult attributes (such as control and judgment), which could inhibit the spontaneity and genuineness of their responses.

Child and adolescent participants will be easily distracted by novel objects in the interview room. Therefore, the room should be kept as bare as possible, and equipment (e.g., microphones) being used should be placed out of view of the participants.

The Moderator Guide

It is still necessary that a moderator guide be prepared when conducting focus groups with children and adolescents. When constructing this guide, one should consider the possible meanings that children and adolescents may attribute to the words selected. For example, an adolescent may consider the popular rap singer's definition for the word *bad*, whereas an adult is more likely to rely upon the word's major denotation. If the moderator guide is pre-tested on participants from the same age group as the actual focus group participants, then any confusing or unfamiliar language will be discovered in time to be clarified before the study. A sample moderator guide for a focus group with children is presented in Table 9.2.

Focus Group Questions and Discussion. It is vital to be concrete for a successful focus group interview with children and adolescents. The questions to be asked of the participants should be stated in clear, simple language, and illustrations should be provided. For example, "How do you feel about your mainstreamed classmates?" is a question with jargon that may be unfamiliar to young participants. The above question could be simplified as follows, "What do you think about your classmates who leave the classroom and go to another room for extra help?" The following statements illustrate the use of examples to make certain the participants understand the question: "Some teachers give all their students the same test. Other teachers change their tests for some students, for example, by making the test shorter or easier, by reading the test questions out loud, or by translating the test into another language. Which kind of teacher would you prefer and why?" Asking children negative questions (e.g., What do you *not* like about your social studies class?) before asking a positive question relays the message that it is acceptable to talk about negative aspects or criticisms (Spethmann, 1992). This is a particularly important point to stress because the focus group is interested in the participants' real experiences and not an artificially rosy picture.

Moderators who work with children and adolescents must sometimes probe the participants' comprehension to check that they understood the questions or issues presented. Consider, for example, "Would someone repeat the question I just asked but in different words?" or "Who can tell me what the school counselor does?" From the participants' responses to such questions, the moderator will know whether the general topics and specific questions of the focus group interview are understood by the participants or whether further explanations are needed before an appropriate focus group discussion can begin.

Opening the Focus Group Interview

The moderator's opening remarks should take into consideration the age group of the participants. If, for example, the participants are young children, then the moderator need only explain the general reason for the focus group (e.g., to help their teachers understand more about how students learn, or to help doctors learn about the concerns of children). When the participants are older children or adolescents, however, a more sophisticated description is in order. With these participants, it is appropriate to identify the agency or department sponsoring the focus group interview as well as the reason the focus group is being conducted. Although children will not comprehend the research behind the focus group interview,

Sample Moderator's Guide for a Focus Group With Child
Participants

*"Hello girls. My name is Tiffany and I work at the University of
interested in learning about your experiences in school. All of you are
grade but in different classrooms. In a few minutes, I'm going to ask you
stions about your schools, classrooms, teachers, and classmates. There
are no wrong answers to the questions I will ask you. I just want to hear what you
think or feel about the questions I ask. Also, you will not be graded on your
answers. In fact, your teachers, your parents, and your classmates will not know
how you answered any of the questions I will ask. If you have any questions about
what I just said, please raise your hand now."*

"Okay, when I ask a question you don't *have to raise your hand to answer. But it
is very important that I hear all of your answers. So when you have something to
say, please wait until the person talking stops talking or until I call your name. I
want you to remember one last thing before we begin. Some of you may agree with
some of the answers you hear others saying, and you may disagree with some of
the other answers people give. It is important that you let me know when you
agree and when you disagree with each other. Are there any questions about this?"*

[Allow a couple minutes for questions and answers.]

Warm-up *"Let's introduce ourselves. I would like each of you to say your first name
and to tell us what you drew on your name tag while you were in the waiting room.
I'll start. My name is Tiffany and I drew a picture of a big, yellow sun on my name
tag. Now, let's go around the table starting here (point to girl on moderator's left), and
you say your first name and tell us what you drew on your name tag."*

[Allow each girl a moment to say her name and to describe her name tag
drawing.]

Clarification of Terms *"I am going to ask you questions about your participation
in your classes. When I use the word participation, what I mean is activities like
volunteering answers to teachers' questions or volunteering to go up to the
blackboard and write an answer to a problem or question. Could someone give me
another example of what I mean by participation in class?"*

[Explain why a given example is right or wrong and continue to solicit
examples until two correct ones have been said.]

"Are there any questions about participation? Okay, then here is my first question."

Questions
  1. How do you feel about participating in your class?
     Probe: Allow each girl to respond.
     Probe: Do you feel the same way about participating in all of your classes?
     If no, in which classes is the feeling different and why?

TABLE 9.2 Continued

2. What kinds of things do you have to do to get your teacher to call on you in class?
   Probe: When do you do these things?
   Probe: When do these things *not* work?

3. Are there kids in your class who get called on without trying?
   Probe: Describe their behaviors or characteristics.

4. How do you feel about the kids in your class who participate the most?

5. Are there things you do so you *won't* get called on in class?
   Probe: What do you do exactly?
   Probe: How does the teacher respond?
   Probe: How do you feel when you do these things?

6. Are there things your teacher could do that would make you want to participate more?
   Probe: What are these things exactly?
   Probe: Why are these things not being done now?

7. Are there things your classmates could do that would make you want to participate more?
   Probe: Whate these things exactly?
   Probe: Why are these things not being done now?

Wrap-Up *"Unfortunately, we are almost out of time. Let me repeat the main points you gave in your responses."*

[Identify the major themes of the participants' responses and summarize them.]

Member Check *"I am going to ask each of you how you feel about some of the big issues that we have just talked about. We are not going to discuss these points like we did the questions I just asked you. Instead, I just want you to tell me your feelings about the issue."*

Closing Statement *"I want to thank all of you very much for coming here and talking with me today. I really enjoyed meeting all of you, and your answers have really helped me better understand what school is like for you. Again, I want to remind you that your teachers, parents, and classmates will not know your answers. Do you have any last questions?"*

[Allow a couple of minutes for questions and answers.]

"Okay, now if you will follow me, I will show you where your parents are waiting to take you home. And thank you again for helping me today."

adolescents will likely take pride in and become more motivated by being asked to participate in a research project in which their individual experiences are valued by others.

The process of obtaining spontaneous and genuine responses in focus groups begins with making the participants feel comfortable. Children and some adolescents will likely enter the focus group believing their participation is going to be evaluated in some manner, just as their performance in school is graded. To make these participants feel comfortable, it is important for the moderator to describe at the outset the true purpose of the focus group and to dispel any possible misinformation that the moderator grades or judges the participants' responses or work within the focus group.

Adolescents may have a more difficult time believing that they and their responses are not being evaluated. Because of this, it is often more difficult to establish rapport. The moderator who is open and honest with these participants will be best able to promote a trusting and open atmosphere. It is recommended that the moderator ask the participants how they feel about being a part of the focus group and then validate their responses. Also, attempts should be made to fully explain the importance of the participants' responses and that their perspective on the topic is both unique and valuable.

The moderator should explain that the focus group interview is aimed at better understanding what the children think, feel, and experience and that there are no wrong answers. It is beneficial for the moderator to further explain that the participants shouldn't "copy" each other's responses but, instead, should answer what is true for them even if it is different from other participants' answers. These comments serve to motivate the children for two reasons. First, the children learn that they are not being evaluated, thereby eliminating the pressure to meet certain standards. Second, the moderator's genuine interest in listening to the children's experiences boosts their feelings of importance.

Children are also made to feel more comfortable when the focus group begins by engaging them in some form of enjoyable and easily mastered activity. For example, in one series of focus group interviews with 8- to 10-year olds, the children were encouraged to imitate the moderator (e.g., clapping hands, jumping in place; McDonald & Topper, 1988). Engaging the children in activities that they would likely see as fun and that are readily mastered served to (a) let the children have fun with and enjoy the focus group interview, (b) allay any concerns the children may have about not participating appropriately or sufficiently (especially compared to their cohorts), and (c) get the children engaged in the group process. To stay interested and focused during the interview, children require more stimulation in the environment and more interaction on the part of the moderator than do adult participants. As a result, whenever activities (e.g., drawing on sketch pads, role playing, writing) can be introduced into the focus group interview, the activities will serve to spice up the interview and to help maintain attention. In addition, some children may be better able to express themselves through a nonverbal medium or through unstructured exercises. These can be followed up and probed by the moderator in the same ways as other participant responses.

Introducing the Participants. Younger participants (as well as the moderator) should wear name tags. With very young children, part of the opening activities could include coloring and drawing on the name tags and then, in turn, describing what they drew. Participants of any age will be curious about why they were selected to participate. The moderator should explain what the participants have in common (e.g., they all are sophomores in high school, or they all are in a gifted program in their schools).

The Role of Parents/Guardians

In order to include any individual under the age of 18 years in a focus group interview, it is necessary to gain permission from that individual's parent or guardian. During the initial contact with a parent or guardian, the researcher should explain (a) the purpose of the focus group interviews, (b) the importance of the participation by that particular child, (c) the extent to which the child's responses will be kept confidential, (d) the commitment that participation entails, and (e) any compensation that the child (or parent/guardian) might receive in exchange for participating. When arranging the time and location of the focus group interview, consider the constraints on the parent/guardian as well as on the child or adolescent. For example, scheduling a focus group interview on the same evening as a PTA (Parent-Teacher Association) meeting or during the workday will likely preclude the participation of those children whose participation is dependent on being brought to (and from) the focus group site.

In addition, the adults will need a comfortable room in which to wait for their children during the focus group interview. The room should be equipped with a television or several magazines and newspapers as well as light refreshments (e.g., coffee, soft drinks, and crackers). Parents and guardians will likely be cautious about leaving their children alone at the focus group site with the moderator and others who are strangers. When the participants arrive at the focus group site, the moderator should introduce him- or herself to the parents or guardians, including in the introduction his or her credentials. The moderator should also answer any questions that the parents or guardians may have. By asking the parents or guardians to escort their children into the focus group interview room, they will become familiar with the focus group setting. This also helps those children who are more dependent on their parents or guardians to adjust to the unfamiliar surroundings.

Games should be available so the children will be kept interested while they wait for other participants to arrive and for the parents to be settled. Games that have a specific beginning and ending (e.g., board games) should be avoided as children may be upset if the start of the interview interrupts the game. Instead, art materials, blank paper, and manipulative toys are recommended. As the children begin to play, the adults should be escorted to the waiting room.

Ethical Considerations

If the children's parents or guardians provide consent, their teachers or clinicians are supportive of the research project, and a researcher with vested interests in the children's participation in the project requests their assent, to what extent are the children free to dissent? As emphasized in this question, children are commonly perceived as being particularly vulnerable when serving as research participants because of their lack of social power. And, unfortunately, no clear answers exist for all of the moral dilemmas that arise in research with young children. Considering the ethic guidelines of several professional organizations in psychology an education (e.g., American Psychological Association, Council for Exceptional Children), we recommend that researchers treat children with the same respect and understanding as they would adults. Therefore, the same principles that apply in conducting research with adults apply when determining the appropriateness of using children as research participants. The basic principle is to "do no harm" to the participant. For children—who may not recognize the benefits of participating in research—this frequently means minimizing potentially stressful situations within the research settings. This requires examining the research environment and protocol from the *perspective of the participant* and taking into account the importance of informed consent. Table 9.3 is a sample informal consent form for children.

TABLE 9.3 Sample Informed Consent Form for Children

Student Informed Consent Form

I, _____ ,

(print your name)

have been told that the University of Miami is doing a project on how elementary school children feel about school, their teachers, and other children in their class. I have been asked to be part of this project. Students who agree to be part of the project will complete certain questionnaires. They will also be interviewed in groups by someone from the university. Finally, someone from the university will look up my grades and test scores.

I know that whether or not I take part in the project is up to me and that whatever I decide will not affect my grades or what my teacher thinks of me. No one except people working on the project at the University of Miami will know how I answered any questions, and they will not report my answers by my name. I know that the papers with my answers will be kept without my name on them until the university finishes the project. I also know that even if I decide to be part of the project now, I can change my mind at any time and this will not affect my grades or anything else at school.

I want to be part of this project. I agree to fill out some questionnaires, to be interviewed, and to let people working on the project look up my grades and test scores.

_____   _____

Sign your name   Date

An important consideration in psychology and education is the extent to which involving selected children in research "marks" them as different and brings undue attention to them. For example, when students who perform poorly are removed from a classroom to participate in a research study, this could contribute to interpersonal and intrapersonal conflicts, the results of which could linger far beyond the end of the research project. Overall, it is recommended that researchers respect the beliefs, attitudes, wishes, and rights (including the right to refuse participation) of prospective participants, regardless of their ages.

ACTIVITIES

1. Develop study questions for which you would use focus group interviews with children or adolescents as the participants. What specific modifications in (a) the moderator's guide, (b) the facility, and (c) the discussion would you make in order to maximize the potential effectiveness of the focus groups with the population you selected?

2. Compare and contrast the transcript from a focus group interview with adult participants with the transcript from a focus group interview with child/adolescent participants. Keep the following questions in mind: (a) What similarities and differences do you detect? (b) In what ways did the moderator ensure that the participants understood the interview questions? and (c) In what ways did the moderator keep the participants focused?

3. Interview a researcher who has extensive experience working with children and/or adolescents. Identify the skills necessary to work effectively with these populations.

4. Prepare a moderator's guide for a mock focus group interview with either children or adolescents. (It may be the guide from your questions in Activity 1.) Pretest the moderator's guide on individuals from the designated age group. How appropriate was the language in your moderator's guide to the comprehension level of the participants? What changes would you make before using this guide in an actual focus group interview?

POTENTIAL ABUSES OF
FOCUS GROUP INTERVIEWS

OVERVIEW

The prospects for understanding human phenomena using focus group interviews are great but not limitless. Misunderstood or misused focus groups are potentially dangerous. Indeed, focus group interviews have been criticized on a number of grounds, including questionable sampling procedures, infusion of moderator bias during the interview, lack of "hard data," and inability to generalize findings. Many of these criticisms are warranted if the focus group interview is inappropriate for the research purpose or questions or if it is not conducted and interpreted within the confines of its limitations.

Focus groups are an efficient and effective means for gathering in-depth qualitative data. However, in considering the uses of focus group interviews, the researcher must also appraise the potential misuse of the research tool. If basic assumptions are violated, if focus groups are not compatible with the intended approach and research questions, or if key players are unable or unwilling to participate, then other research strategies should be explored.

Wells (1974) wrote about the technique, "How can anything so bad be good?" (p. 2). Our personal experiences in using this research methodology have led us to recognize the merit of focus group interviews for research in education and psychology. We have found that, when properly administered, they yield data that are rich and insightful. Our experiences and our reading of the literature have also helped us recognize that there are common misunderstandings about the purpose and use of focus groups and that these misunderstandings can lead to misuse.

CHAPTER 10

KEY IDEAS IN THIS CHAPTER

◆ Although focus groups can yield rich, in-depth data, the potential for abuse is possible before, during, and after the conduct of the interview.

◆ Focus groups are simply inappropriate for some research purposes.

◆ Focus groups are highly dependent on the quality of interactions of the moderator and participants.

◆ The potential for contamination of data during the interview is high.

◆ Data analysis and interpretation are complex and time-consuming.

◆ Particular caution needs to be exerted when considering generalizability of findings.

Potential Misuses Before
the Conduct of the Focus Group

The logical first step in launching any investigation in psychology or education should be the development of a clearly defined research plan. The decision to employ any research tool is dependent on the goodness-of-fit between the research tool and the purposes and design of the study as detailed in the research plan. In making the initial decision to use a focus group interview, the researcher must consider if it is the best tool for answering the designated research questions. Sample questions for which focus group interviews alone would not be the appropriate research methodology are presented in Table 10.1.

Moreover, because the success of the focus group is dependent on the availability of an appropriate sample and a trained moderator, these factors must also be appraised. Such considerations are vital in enabling the researcher to avoid potential misuses of focus group interviews.

APPLICABILITY

One of the greatest abuses of focus group interviews is employing them as a research tool when they are incompatible with the research questions and design. Stewart and Shamdasani (1990) noted,

> There are those who would use focus groups to explore all manner of research questions. This view, however, is as inappropriate as the view that dismisses the focus group as having no utility. The focus group is one tool in the social scientist's research tool kit and it should be used where it is appropriate and for the purposes for which it was designed. . . . There is an unfortunate tendency among some social scientists to view the world in the same way. Thus, they tend to regard focus groups as either appropriate or inappropriate, sound or unsound, without regard to the research question. (p. 18)

Simply put, focus group interviews are not applicable for some research purposes. As McQuarrie and McIntyre (1987) stated, "Fo-

TABLE 10.1 Questions Inappropriate for Investigations Using Focus Group Interviews as the Sole Research Method

1. Does awareness of narrating patterns transfer from the reader's first language to his or her second language?

2. Does frequent exposure to violent films increase the number of student referrals for disciplinary action in secondary schools?

3. How frequently do mathematics concepts appear in preschool children's spontaneous play?

4. Does an interactive reading comprehension strategy improve the quality of student recall of written reading to a greater degree than traditional comprehension instruction?

5. Which of two conflict resolution strategies is most effective in improving young children's relationships with siblings?

6. What is the prevalence of home literacy activities among new Hispanic immigrants?

7. How many students who speak English as a second language are inappropriately identified as learning disabled?

8. How many classroom teachers have had professional development in teaching students with high-incidence disabilities?

9. What is the frequency of sexual intimacy among teenagers in a suburban high school?

cus groups are very good at what they do; but they cannot do everything" (p. 59). Focus group interviews are unsuitable for a variety of purposes:

- Testing hypotheses in traditional experimental designs
- Drawing inferences from larger populations
- Providing information that is useful for statistical testing
- Exploring topics that are too intimate or sensitive for group interviews.

Even when focus group interviews appear to be a logical selection for a designated research purpose, caution must be exercised. As discussed in previous chapters, focus group interviews are appropriate for exploratory research. Focus groups can often provide preliminary information, which can be useful to further design and to explicate future research studies. Nonetheless, to approach a focus group without a clear idea of what information is wanted from the views and perceptions of participants is unlikely to be of any value.

STRUCTURE

Another common abuse of focus groups is inadequate planning for the interview. Because groups are informal, some researchers consider that there is no need to plan the questions and probes. We maintain that a specific plan for the focus group (including target questions and follow-up probes) is necessary for the successful conduct of a focus group.

COST

Focus group interviews should not be designated as the research tool of choice based solely on cost. A very common misunderstanding about focus group interviews is that they are inexpensive or cheap. Certainly, with focus group interviews, the expenses of developing and refining survey instruments, mass mailings, and extensive follow-ups are circumvented. Similarly, data entry and statistical analyses are not involved (Bloch, 1992).

Many are lured into selecting focus group interviews by claims in the literature of their low relative cost. Nonetheless, the cost of focus group interviews, although not readily apparent, can be substantial. If focus group interviews are conducted on a particular topic (e.g., the effectiveness of mathematics interventions), it is often necessary to conduct three or more focus groups that include 8 to 10 people. If each person is provided an honorarium given the amount of time it takes to arrange the focus groups, the groups can be expensive, both in terms of personnel and stipends awarded. There is also the cost of the moderator, the audiotapes and videotapes, the refreshments, and the amount of time and effort it takes to recruit subjects, make arrangements, and transcribe and analyze data. Although many descriptions from the business and marketing perspectives view focus groups as inexpensive, we in education and psychology would view them as a relatively expensive methodology.

TABLE 10.2 Potential Budget Items for Focus Groups

Personnel
    Recruiters
    Moderator
    Assistant moderator
    Transcribers
    Data coders

Participant Recruitment/Incentives
    Postage/mailing
    FAX expenses
    Cash stipends/travel reimbursement
    Child care for participants' youngsters
    Refreshments

Equipment and Supplies
    Audio/video equipment and tapes
    Transcribing machines
    Software for qualitative data analysis

Table 10.2 provides a list of items to be considered in developing a budget for focus groups.

ROLE OF THE MODERATOR

Because the use and application of focus group interviews are often considered to be soft and fuzzy, the perception is that anyone can do it (Bers, 1989). Because the moderator's skills are essential to the success of the focus group, this assumption is quite faulty. Focus group research is both an art and a science (Bers, 1989), and many well-designed focus groups have been spoiled by a less than well-trained, effective moderator.

Another misunderstanding is that focus groups can be conducted by anyone who has even a preliminary understanding of research. Because focus group interviews need trained moderators who understand the dynamics of group interaction, even persons with experience in conducting one-to-one interviews will not automatically be successful in the conduct of a focus group. Even with extensive training in research, an individual may have more experience with computers than people. As Bers (1989) states, "Many are also [more] accustomed to reporting results than listening for ideas" (p. 264). Unfortunately, the procedures for the expert conduct of focus groups are infrequently taught in traditional research classes. Sufficient time to identify and prepare moderators for the interviews is critical, and analysis and interpretation of data take insight and expertise. Therefore, focus group interviews are not for the novice or inexperienced researcher.

DID YOU KNOW THAT?

Bers (1989) cautioned that breaches of research ethics can arise in the use of professional focus group moderators. Because no certification or specific training is required, individuals can claim to possess expertise they simply do not have. Bers recommends a thorough check with previous clients before a professional moderator is engaged.

PARTICIPANTS

Focus group interviews typically involve purposive sampling. The research issues are identified, and individuals whose points of view are most salient are invited to participate. For example, in an examination of college students' perceptions of strategies taught in a study skills course, separate focus group interviews may be conducted with students typically enrolled in the class (e.g., international students, students with learning disabilities, students with low grade point averages after the first semester).

Compared to traditional sampling and subject recruitment in large-scale studies, this procedure sounds extraordinarily straightforward, but this simplicity can be deceiving. Recruiting subjects is not always as easy as one might expect. Even after potential subjects have been screened and identified, the logistics of finding a common meeting time are complex. Consequently, a potential abuse of focus group interviews is the failure to allocate sufficient time and effort in identifying appropriate participants—resulting in the temptation to resort to "convenience" samples. The use of samples that are less than desirable could result, ultimately, in abandonment of the project.

Another danger is the potential reluctance to participate by some worthwhile, yet vulnerable, target populations. Many members of the general public mistrust research. This mistrust can stem from cultural differences; prior experiences; or the unfamiliar, distant, and perhaps threatening domain from which research emanates. As Basch (1987) observed, "Potentially valuable contributors such as people with hearing or speech problems, very young and very old individuals, and people intimidated by articulating their views in public are likely to be excluded" (pp. 432-433).

Potential Misuses During the Conduct of the Focus Group

ATMOSPHERE

A common misunderstanding about the conduct of focus groups is that they are "loose" and not precise in the way they are conducted and organized. Although the interview often gives the impression of being casual and "informal" conversation, it is actually the result of a highly planned session with clearly identified objectives and carefully composed questions.

DID YOU KNOW THAT?

One of the most common mistakes of novice focus group moderators is to adhere tenaciously to predetermined questions. Calder (1977) recommended the avoidance of "serial questions where a number of people are simply being interviewed at once. Interaction among the participants is held up as the basic rationale for the technique" (p. 362).

Although the intent of focus group interviews is to create an informal ambiance that will elicit and encourage participation, it should not be forgotten that the focus group is an unnatural setting for most subjects (Morgan & Spanish, 1984). McQuarrie and McIntyre (1987) have countered that this argument could be made for any survey or interview-type research. Nonetheless, the moderator should be vigilant about putting participants at ease and constantly aware that the setting is unnatural. Participants will not have the opportunity to be articulate and authentic or to otherwise participate fully if (a) the general environment of the interview is threatening, (b) the questions are inappropriate or ambiguous, or (c) the moderator is inept in eliciting and encouraging responses or disrespectful of the integrity of responses. The danger of thwarting the responses of participants is particularly threatening when conducting focus group interviews with children and when there is an inconsistency between the culture or language of the moderator and the participants.

PARTICIPANT-MODERATOR INTERACTION

The focus group interview depends on intensive interactions between key players: the moderator with the participants and the participants with each other. On the other hand, abuses of focus groups and opportunities for contamination of data are a consequence of these interactions.

First, although subjects may be more open about a topic with the support of a group, the pull for socially desirable responses cannot be ignored. As Byers and Wilcox (1988) observed, "Participants in the focus group may provide answers which they believe are socially acceptable so as not to appear abnormal or deviant from the other group members" (p. 13). Consider, for instance, a focus group interview of college students to determine their perceptions of cheating practices. Participants' willingness to provide candid responses is likely to be influenced by many factors, including the makeup of the focus group membership, assurances of confidentiality of responses, and how interview questions are worded.

Second, perhaps the greatest danger to the openness of responses is the infusion of bias during the interviews. The moderator, a strong participant, or the dynamic of the group may introduce a particular perspective that inhibits active participation from participants who are less powerful or less vocal. For example, in a focus group interview of individuals who claim to have repressed memories of childhood sexual abuse, a researcher/moderator who questions the authenticity of recovered memories may infuse bias through the wording of questions and prompts, through responses to participant comments, or by allowing a participant whose personal experience affirms the bias to dominate the conversation.

Finally, focus group interviews must be conducted with the assumptions that individuals do not necessarily come to the interviews with well-defined, unalterable opinions on topics, that participants may actually shape their opinions during the interview, and that the primary intent of the interviews must not be to coerce or intimidate participants into espousing a particular point of view. For example, a focus group interview of parents of gay and lesbian young adults to determine their perceptions of same-sex marriages would not yield candid results if the participants detected that the moderator was trying to promote a particular stance on the issue. Similarly, representatives from opposing points of view should not be invited as focus group participants with the intent of reaching consensus on an issue. The purpose of focus group interviews is to gather data: It is not to educate, persuade, or mediate.

Potential Misuses After
Conduct of the Focus Group

DATA ANALYSIS AND INTERPRETATION

Another false assumption about focus groups that can lead to abuse is that the data are easy to analyze and the findings are readily apparent. It often takes an extensive amount of time to summarize, analyze, and identify common themes that are agreed on by several analysts. Although some key findings are apparent, some of the more subtle findings take more time and require extensive sifting and examination of the data.

Interpretation of data is not always as straightforward as one might think. This is particularly true when coding data from written transcripts. To illustrate this point, we prepared an initial summarization of data from a written transcript of a focus group interview of teachers regarding their feelings about including students with disabilities in their general education classrooms. Subsequent research meetings, which included focus group moderators, revealed that the strength of the teachers' concerns about this practice were not readily apparent in the written transcript nor in the summary of data. Written transcripts can be interpreted inaccurately if participants' nonverbal responses are not attended to and recorded in some way—either from the field notes of observers or from notes made of the videotapes. Intonations, facial expressions, body language, and frequency of participation need to be considered when interpreting results.

GENERALIZABILITY OF RESULTS

As in the case of much of qualitative research, one of the major issues with focus group interviews is the generalizability of results. The intent of focus group interviews is to report the views of participants, not to generalize to larger groups. Indeed, one of the potential misuses of focus groups is to project findings to a larger population. One example is the statement, "Six out of ten parents participating in a focus group interview agreed that the annual administration of standardized achievement tests by a school district should be eliminated. Therefore, it is safe to conclude that a reasonable majority of the parents in the school district would share a similar view." As McQuarrie and McIntyre (1987) have argued, it is a gross misuse to project an incidence of responses based on findings from a focus group interview. Byers and Wilcox (1991) advised that the goal of focus groups should be to find out *why* rather than *how many*.

In lieu of incidence generalization from focus group interviews, McQuarrie and McIntyre (1987) recommended as a more appropriate goal the "domain of response type of generalization" (p. 59). These authors suggested that during the course of a focus group discussion, group members identify salient concepts related to an issue. Some of the concepts might be (a) typical responses of a larger population, (b) typical responses of a particular subgroup, and (c) highly individual and idiosyncratic responses. The group discussion can help discriminate these types of responses to lead to a "near census" of salient common responses, particularly when multiple focus group interviews on a single issue are conducted.

As Brotherson (1994) stated, "Qualitative research does not have as a goal 'truth statements,' but rather descriptions of patterns present in the data so that other investigators can make decisions about the 'fit' or match of those patterns to other contexts" (p. 115). Similarly, Bers (1987) observed, "The method is best used to identify attitudinal dimensions and not to quantify the extent to which these are held in any population or subgroup" (p. 19).

Because the focus group interview puts the researcher in direct contact with representatives of a group of interest, there is a strong potential for misinterpretation of findings. Nonetheless, it is important to remember that focus group interviews often provide the views of key stakeholders, and these can stimulate the thinking of researchers. As long as information garnered from focus group interviews is treated as everyday knowledge rather than as final, generalizable research, it can be very useful. The important goal is to hear the voices and viewpoints of the target individuals.

ACTIVITIES

1. Identify several research topics for which focus group interviews would be inappropriate. Check with your colleagues for their reactions to your selections.

2. You are going to conduct a series of ten focus group interviews. Work with a small group (your research team) to draft a projected budget for the personnel and supplies needed to recruit subjects, train personnel, conduct the interviews, and analyze and interpret data. Compare your budget with those developed by other research teams.

3. Discuss with friends and family members the factors that might encourage or discourage them from volunteering to participate in a focus group interview.

4. Which three of the potential abuses of focus group interviews discussed in this chapter are of greatest concern to you? What other abuses not mentioned in the chapter have occurred to you? Discuss your answers to these questions with a small group of colleagues.

REFERENCES

Antonucci, F. J. (1989). *Maine state plan: Assuring access to education for homeless children and youths* (Report No. UD-027-667). Augusta, MA: Office of Education of Homeless Children and Youth. (ERIC Document Reproduction Service No. ED 326 591)

A step-by-step way to conduct worthwhile focus groups. (1978). *Training, 15*(12), 50, 55.

Baca, P. (1989). *Focusing on re: learning* (Report No. EA-021-909). Denver, CO: Education Commission of the States. (ERIC Document Reproduction Service No. ED 320 256)

Baker, P. N. (1985). Focus group interviewing: The real constituency. *Journal of Data Collection, 25*(2), 14-23.

Basch, C. E. (1987). Focus group interview: An underutilized research technique for improving theory and practice in health education. *Health Education Quarterly, 14*(4), 411-448.

Bauman, L. J., & Adair, E. G. (1992). The use of ethnographic interviewing to inform questionnaire construction. *Health Education Quarterly, 19*(1), 9-23.

Beck, L. C., Trombetta, W. L., & Share, S. (1986). Using focus group sessions before decisions are made. *North Carolina Medical Journal, 47*(2), 73-74.

Bellenger, D. N., Bernhardt, K. L., & Goldstucker, J. L. (1976). Qualitative research techniques: Focus group interviews. In J. B. Higginbotham & K. K. Cox (Eds.), *Focus group interviews: A reader* (pp. 13-28). Chicago: American Marketing Association.

Bennett, A. (1986, June 3). Once a tool of retail marketers, focus groups gain wider usage. *Wall Street Journal*, p. 31.

Bers, T. H. (1987). Exploring institutional images through focus group interviews. *New Directions for Institutional Research, No. 54 (Designing and Using Marketing Research), 14*(2), 19-29.

Bers, T. H. (1989). The popularity and problems of focus-group research. *College and University, 64*, 260-268.

Bertrand, J. T., Brown, J. E., & Ward, V. M. (1992). Techniques for analyzing focus group data. *Evaluation Review, 16*, 198-209.

Bertrand, J. T., Ward, V. M., & Pauc, F. (1992). Sexual practices among the Quiche-speaking Mayan population of Guatemala. *International Quarterly of Community Health Education, 12*, 265-282.

Birnie, B. F. (1988). *Profiles and practices: An investigation of senior high school English teachers selected as Teacher of the Year in Dade County, Florida, 1983-1988.* Unpublished doctoral dissertation, University of Miami.

Black, G. S. (1989). *The lack of confidence in public education in Wisconsin* (Report No. UD-027-233). Milwaukee: Wisconsin Policy Research Institution. (ERIC Document Reproduction Service No. ED 315 472)

Bloch, D. P. (1992). The application of group interviews to the planning and evaluation of career development programs. *Career Development Quarterly, 40,* 340-350.

Bogdan, R., & Biklen, S. K. (1992). *Qualitative research for education: An introduction to theory and methods* (2nd ed.). Boston: Allyn & Bacon.

Borg, W. R., Gall, J. P., & Gall, M. D. (1993). *Applying educational research: A practical guide.* White Plains, NY: Longman.

Bortree, W. H. (1986). Focus groups reduce innovation risks. *Bank Marketing, 18*(11), 18-24.

Brodigan, D. L. (1992). *Focus group interviews: Applications for institutional research* (Report No. HE-025-299). Carleton, MN: Carleton College, Institutional Research. (ERIC Document Reproduction Service No. ED 342 325)

Brotherson, M. J. (1994). Interactive focus group interviewing: A qualitative research method in early intervention. *Topics in Early Childhood Special Education, 14,* 101-118.

Buncher, M. M. (1982, September 17). Focus groups seem easy to do and use, but they're easier to misuse and abuse. *Marketing News,* pp. 14-15.

Buttram, J. L. (1990). *Focus groups: A starting point for needs assessment* (Report No. EA-022-151). Philadelphia: Research for Better Schools, Inc. (ERIC Document Reproduction Service No. ED 322 628)

Buttram, J. L. (1991). *Conversations on school restructuring in the mid-Atlantic region* (Report No. EA-023-399). Philadelphia: Research for Better Schools, Inc. (ERIC Document Reproduction Service No. ED 337 874)

Byers, P. Y., & Wilcox, J. R. (1988). *Focus groups: An alternative method of gathering qualitative data in communication research* (Report No. CS-506-291). New Orleans, LA: Speech Communication Association. (ERIC Document Reproduction Service No. ED 297 393)

Byers, P. Y., & Wilcox, J. R. (1991). Focus groups: A qualitative opportunity for researchers. *Journal of Business Communication, 28,* 63-77.

Calder, B. J. (1977). Focus groups and the nature of qualitative marketing research. *Journal of Marketing Research, 14,* 353-364.

Calder, B. J. (1978, October 20). Surveys' objective: To improve focus group studies. *Marketing News,* pp. 1, 5.

Cannon, A. (1994, April 18). Clinton's love of polls shows he can't stop campaigning, critics say. *Miami Herald,* p. 4A.

Chaubey, N. P. (1974). Effect of age on expectancy of success on risk-taking behavior. *Journal of Personality and Social Psychology, 249,* 774-778.

Cohen, M. C., & Engleberg, I. N. (1989). *Focus group research: Procedures and pitfalls* (Report No. JC-890-247). Ocean City, MD: Eastern Communication Association. (ERIC Document Reproduction Service No. ED 307 001)

Collins, C., Stommel, M., King, S., & Given, C. W. (1991). Assessment of the attitudes of family caregivers toward community services. *The Gerontologist, 31*(6), 756-761.

Connors, L. (1991). *Building community support* (Report No. PS-020-315). Boston: Massachusetts State Department of Education, Bureau of Early Childhood Programs. (ERIC Document Reproduction Service No. ED 341 516)

Cox, K. K., Higgenbotham, J. B., & Burton, J. (1976). Applications of focus group interviews in marketing. *Journal of Marketing, 40,* 77-80.

Dellens, M. (1979). *Math anxiety: What can a learning center do about it?* (Report No. SE-028-640). Waikiki, HI: Western College Reading Association. (ERIC Document Reproduction Service No. ED 176 963)

Durgee, J. (1986, December). Point of view: Using creative writing techniques in focus groups. *Journal of Advertising Research,* 57-65.

Dyson, J. W., Godwin, P. H. B., & Hazelwood, L. A. (1976). Group composition, leadership, orientation, and decisional outcomes. *Small Group Behavior, 7,* 114-128.

Egbert, H. A. (1983, March). Focus groups: A basic tool to probe buyers' attitudes. *Industrial Marketing,* pp. 82, 84.

Elliott, D. B. (1989). *Community college faculty behaviors impacting transfer student success: A qualitative study* (Report No. JC-890-172). San Francisco: American Educational Research Association. (ERIC Document Reproduction Service No. ED 305 952)

Elrod, J. M. (1981). Improving employee relations with focus groups. *Business, 31*(6), 36-38.

Erkut, S., & Fields, J. P. (1987). Focus groups to the rescue. *Training and Development Journal, 4*(10), 74-76.

Fedder, C. J. (1990, January 8). Biz-to-biz focus groups require a special touch: Three factors affect research outcome. *Marketing News,* p. 46.

Fern, E. F. (1982). The use of focus groups for idea generation: The effects of group size, acquaintanceship, and moderator on response quantity and quality. *Journal of Marketing Research, 19,* 1-13.

Folch-Lyon, E., & Trost, J. F. (1981). Conducting focus group sessions. *Studies in Family Planning, 12*(12), 443-449.

Fry, C. L. (1965). Personality and acquisition factors in the development of coordination strategy. *Journal of Personality and Social Psychology, 2,* 403-407.

Glaser, B. G., & Strauss, A. L. (1967). *The discovery of grounded theory strategy for qualitative research.* Hawthorne, NY: Aldine.

Glesne, C., & Peshkin, A. (1992). *Becoming qualitative researchers: An introduction.* White Plains, NY: Longman.

Gold, R. S., & Kelly, M. A. (1991). Cultural sensitivity in AIDS education: A misunderstood concept. *Evaluation and Program Planning, 14,* 221-231.

Goldman, A. E., & McDonald, S. S. (1987). *The group depth interview: Principles and practice.* Englewood Cliffs, NJ: Prentice Hall.

Goodman, R. I. (1984). Focus group interviews in media product testing. *Educational Technology, 24*(8), 39-44.

Gordon, W. (1990, January 8). Ask the right questions, ye shall receive the right moderator. *Marketing News,* pp. 42, 43.

Greenbaum, T. L. (1988). *The practical handbook and guide to focus group research.* Lexington, MA: Lexington Books.

Greenbaum, T. L. (1991a, May 27). Answer to moderator problems starts with asking the right questions. *Marketing News,* pp. 8, 9.

Greenbaum, T. L. (1991b). Outside moderators maximize focus group results. *Public Relations Journal, 9*(2), 31-32.

Hammond, M. (1986). Creative focus groups: Uses and misuses. *Marketing and Media Decisions, 21*(8), 154, 156.

Hamon, R. R., & Thiessen, J. D. (1990). *Coping with the dissolution of an adult child's marriage* (Report No. CG-023-311). Seattle, WA: National Council on Family Relations. (ERIC Document Reproduction Service No. ED 330 968)

Hanson, M. (1991). *Written communication and the marketing of public schools* (Report No. EA-022-942). Chicago: American Educational Research Association. (ERIC Document Reproduction Service No. ED 331 180)

Hess, J. M. (1968). Group interviewing. In R. L. King (Ed.), *New science of planning* (pp. 51-84). Chicago: American Marketing Association.

Hillebrandt, I. S. (1979). Focus group research: Behind the one-way mirror. *Public Relations Journal, 35*(2), 17, 33.

Hisrich, R. D., & Peters, M. P. (1982). Focus groups: An innovative marketing research technique. *Hospital and Health Services Administration, 27*(4), 8-21.

Hughes, M. T., Schumm, J. S., & Vaughn, S. (1994, December). *Hispanic parents' perceptions and practices with respect to home literacy instruction.* Paper presented at the annual meeting of the National Reading Conference, San Diego, CA.

Hyland, M. E., Finnis, S., & Irvine, S. H. (1990). A scale for assessing quality of life in adult asthma sufferers. *Journal of Psychosomatic Research, 35,* 99-110.

Johnston, K., & Crawford, P. (1989). *Student perceptions of the Role of the Reader Project* (Report No. CS-009-927). Willowdale, Ontario: North York Board of Education. (ERIC Document Reproduction Service No. ED 332 146)

Karger, T. (1987, August 28). Focus groups are for focusing, and for little else. *Marketing News,* 52-55.

Kleiner, R. E. (1991). *Assessing the holding power and attractiveness of a school system for at-risk students.* Longmeadow, MA: Dr. Kleiner, consulting psychologist. (ERIC Document Reproduction Service No. ED 319 752)

Krueger, R. A. (1986). Focus group interviewing: A helpful technique for agricultural educators. *The Visitor, 73*(7), 1-4.

Krueger, R. A. (1988). *Focus groups: A practical guide for applied research.* Newbury Park, CA: Sage.

Langer, J. (1992, January 6). 18 Ways to say "shut up!" *Marketing News,* pp. FG-2, FG-15.

Lederman, L. C. (1990). Accessing educational effectiveness: The focus group interview as a technique for data collection. *Communication Education, 38*(2), 117-127.

Lengua, L. J., Roosa, M. W., Schupak-Neuberg, E., Michaels, M. L., Berg, C. N., & Weschler, L. F. (1992). Using focus groups to guide the development of a parenting program for difficult-to-reach, high-risk families. *Family Relations, 41,* 163-168.

Lewis, R. B., Kitano, M. K., & Lynch, E. W. (1992). Psychological intensities in gifted adults. *Roeper Review, 15*(1), 25-31.

Lincoln, Y. S., & Guba, E. G. (1985). *Naturalistic inquiry.* Beverly Hills, CA: Sage.

Lindgren, J. H., & Kehoe, W. J. (1981). Focus groups: Approaches, procedures and implications. *Journal of Retail Banking, 3*(4), 16-22.

Lyons, L. (1991). *The integration of qualitative and quantitative research in a longitudinal retention study* (Report No. HE-024-854). Jersey City, NJ: Jersey City State College, Institutional Research. (ERIC Document Reproduction Service No. ED 336 034)

Marsiglia, F. F., & Halasa, O. (1992). *Ethnic identity and school achievement as perceived by a group of selected mainland Puerto Rican students* (Report No. UD-028-824). San Francisco: American Educational Research Association. (ERIC Document Reproduction Service No. ED 348 453)

Mates, D., & Allison, R. (1992). Sources of stress and coping responses of high school students. *Adolescence, 27*(105), 461-474.

Maxwell, J. (1992). Understanding and validity in qualitative research. *Harvard Educational Review, 62*(3), 279-300.

Mays, V. M., Cochran, S. D., & Bellinger, G. (1992). The language of black gay men's sexual behavior: Implications for AIDS risk reduction. *Journal of Sex Research, 29*(3), 425-434.

McCormick, W. (1987). *Delaware's report on early childhood education 1987: Findings and recommendations of the Governor's early childhood education study committee* (Report No. PS-017-844). Dover: Delaware State Department of Public Instruction. (ERIC Document Reproduction Service No. ED 304 239)

McDonald, W. J., & Topper, G. E. (1988). Focus-group research with children: A structural approach. *Applied Marketing Research, 28,* 3-11.

McQuarrie, E. F., & McIntyre, S. H. (1987). What focus groups can and cannot do: A reply to Seymour. *Journal of Product Innovation Management, 4,* 55-60.

Mehrabian, A., & Diamond, S. G. (1971). Effects of furniture arrangement, props, and personality on social interaction. *Journal of Personality and Social Psychology, 20,* 18-30.

Merton, R. K. (1987). The focused interview and focus groups: Continuities and discontinuities. *Public Opinion Quarterly, 51*(4), 550-556.

Merton, R. K., & Kendall, P. L. (1946). The focused interview. *American Journal of Sociology, 51,* 541-557.

Miles, M. B., & Huberman, A. M. (1994). *Qualitative data analysis: An expanded sourcebook* (2nd ed.). Thousand Oaks, CA: Sage.

Miller, W. J. (1987). *Focus group study of teachers' perceptions of the instructional program for reading language arts and instruction in mathematics curricula* (Report No. TM-012-031). Rockville, MD: Montgomery County Public Schools, Department of Educational Accountability. (ERIC Document Reproduction Service No. ED 300 369)

Morgan, D. L. (1988). *Focus groups as qualitative research.* Newbury Park, CA: Sage.

Morgan, D. L., & Krueger, R. A. (1993). When to use focus groups and why. In D. L. Morgan (Ed.), *Successful focus groups: Advancing the state of the art* (pp. 3-19). Newbury Park, CA: Sage.

Morgan, D. L., & Spanish, M. T. (1984). Focus groups: A new tool for qualitative research. *Qualitative Sociology, 7*(3), 253-270.

National Association for Independent Colleges and Universities. (1991). *Thank you for asking! Using focus groups to improve minority participation* (Report No. UD-028-570). Washington, DC: National Association of Independent Colleges and Universities. (ERIC Document Reproduction Service No. ED 342 862)

Nelson, J. E., & Frontczak, N. T. (1988). How acquaintanceship and analyst can influence focus group results. *Journal of Advertising, 17,* 41-48.

Nolan, M. J., & Petersen, K. K. (1992). Gender differences in parent-child communication about sexuality: An exploratory study. *Journal of Adolescent Research, 7*(1), 59-79.

Packard, F. D., & Dereshiwsky, M. I. (1990). *Evaluation research: Assessment of a rural Arizona school district using a case study model for single-setting, embedded focus group interview & analysis procedures* (Report No. TM-015-545). Flagstaff: Northern Arizona University, Center for Excellence in Education. (ERIC Document Reproduction Service No. ED 324 332)

Patterson, L., Santa, C. M., Short, K. G., & Smith, K. H. (Eds.). (1993). *Teachers are researchers: Reflection and action.* Newark, DE: International Reading Association.

Patton, M. Q. (1980). *Qualitative evaluation methods.* Beverly Hills, CA: Sage.

Patton, M. Q. (1990). *Qualitative evaluation methods* (2nd ed.). Newbury Park, CA: Sage.

Quiriconi, R. J., & Dorgan, R. E. (1985). Respondent personalities: Insight for better focus groups. *Journal of Data Collection, 25*(2), 20-23.

Redfield, D. L., & Craig, J. R. (1988). *Parents and students as stakeholders in the teacher evaluation process* (Report No. TM-011-425). New Orleans, LA: American Educational Research Association. (ERIC Document Reproduction Service No. ED 293 859)

Reitan, H. T., & Shaw, M. E. (1964). Group membership, sex-composition of the group, and conformity behavior. *Journal of Social Psychology, 64,* 45-51.

Reynolds, F. D., & Johnson, D. K. (1978). Validity of focus-group findings. *Advertising Research, 18*(3), 21-24.

Ringo, S. A. (1992, January 6). Only a real pro has skills to be a moderator. *Marketing News,* pp. FG-1, FG-2.

Rosenstein, A. J. (1976, May 21). Quantitative-yes, quantitative-applications for the focus group, or what do you mean you never heard of "multivariate focus groups?" *Marketing News,* p. 8.

Ruhe, J. A. (1978, May). Effect of leader sex and leader behavior on group problem solving. *Proceedings of the American Institute for Decision Sciences, 1,* (Northeast Division), 123-127.

Sapolsky, A. (1960). Effect of interpersonal relationships upon verbal conditioning. *Journal of Abnormal and Social Psychology, 60,* 241-246.

Schoenfeld, G. (1988, May 23). Unfocus and learn more. *Advertising Age,* p. 20.

Schumm, J. S., Leavell, A. G., Gordon, J., & Murfin, P. (1993). Literacy episodes: What we have learned from undergraduate tutors and at-risk elementary students. *Florida Reading Quarterly, 29*(3), 11-19.

Schumm, J. S., & Vaughn, S. (1991). Making adaptations for mainstreamed students: General classroom teachers' perspectives. *Remedial and Special Education, 12*(4), 18-27.

Schumm, J. S., Vaughn, S., Elbaum, B., & Moody, S. (1995, April). *Teachers' perceptions of grouping practices for reading instruction.* Paper presented at the annual meeting of the American Educational Research Association, San Francisco.

Schumm, J. S., Vaughn, S., Haager, D., McDowell, J. A., Rothlein, L., & Saumell, L. (1995). General education teacher planning: What can students with learning disabilities expect? *Exceptional Children, 61,* 335-352.

Schumm, J. S., Vaughn, S., & Leavell, A. G. (1995). Curricular planning for inclusive classrooms: Three teachers' journeys. Manuscript submitted for publication.

Schumm, J. S., Vaughn, S., & Saumell, L. (1992). What teachers do when the textbook is tough: Students speak out. *Journal of Reading Behavior, 24* (4), 481-503.

Schuster, C. S., & Ashburn, S. S. (1992). *The process of human development: A holistic approach* (3rd ed.). Philadelphia: J. B. Lippincott.

Smelser, W. T. (1961). Dominance as a factor in achievement and perception in cooperative problem solving interactions. *Journal of Abnormal and Social Psychology, 62*, 535-542.

Smith, K. H. (1977). Small group interaction at various ages: Simultaneous talking and interruption of others. *Small Group Behavior, 8*, 65-74.

Spethmann, B. (1992, February 10). Focus groups key to reaching kids. *Advertising Age*, pp. S-1, S-24.

Stewart, D. W., & Shamdasani, P. N. (1990). *Focus groups: Theory and practice.* Newbury Park, CA: Sage.

Strother, R. D. (1984, July 2). Voters' bias shuts door on female leaders. *Minneapolis Star and Tribune*, p. 9A.

Stycos, J. M. (1981). A critique of focus group and survey research: The machismo case. *Studies in Family Planning, 12* (12), 450-456.

Vaughn, S., Klingner, J., & Schumm, J. S. (1994, March). *Comprehension strategy instruction for heterogeneous classrooms.* Paper presented at the annual meeting of the American Educational Research Association, New Orleans, LA.

Vaughn, S., Schumm, J. S., Jallad, B., Slusher, J., & Saumell, L. (in press). Teachers' views of inclusion. *Learning Disabilities Research and Practice.*

Vaughn, S., Schumm, J. S., & Kouzekanani, K. (1993). What do students with learning disabilities think when their general education teachers make adaptations? *Journal of Learning Disabilites, 26*(8), 545-555.

Vaughn, S., Schumm, J. S., Niarhos, F. J., & Gordon, J. (1993). Students' perceptions of two hypothetical teachers' instructional adaptations for low achievers. *Elementary School Journal, 94*, 87-102.

Wells, W. D. (1974). Group interviewing. In J. B. Higginbotham & K. K. Cox (Eds.), *Focus group interviews: A reader* (pp. 2-12). Chicago: American Marketing Association.

Wolf, K. P. (1991). *Research design for investigating the effects of student portfolios on teaching and learning* (Report No. TM-017-336). San Francisco: Far West Laboratory for Educational Research and Development. (ERIC Document Reproduction Service No. ED 337 495)

Yin, R. K. (1989). *Case study research: Design and methods.* Newbury Park, CA: Sage.

Yoell, W. A. (1974). How useful is focus group interviewing? Not very . . . post-interviews reveal. *Marketing Review, 29*, 15-19.

Yuhas, P. L. (1986). *Romantic marital jealousy: An exploratory analysis.* Unpublished doctoral dissertation, Bowling Green State University, Ohio.

Zeller, R. A. (1986). *The focus group: Sociological applications.* Unpublished manuscript, Bowling Green State University, Ohio.

Author Index

Adair, E. G., 26, 28
Allison, R., 27
Antonucci, F. J., 30
Ashburn, S. S., 132

Baca, P., 24
Baker, P. N., 2
Basch, C. E., 9, 27, 59, 71, 101, 151
Bauman, L. J., 26, 28
Beck, L. C., 4, 7, 8, 19, 53, 72
Bellenger, D. N., 2, 84
Bellinger, G., 24
Bennett, A., 69
Bernhardt, K. L., 2
Bers, T. H., 32, 72, 83, 103, 149, 150, 155
Bertrand, J. T., 29, 104, 107
Biklen, S. K., 98
Birnie, B. F., 86, 93
Black, G. S., 31
Bloch, D. P., 148
Bogdan, R., 98
Borg, W. R., 58
Bortree, W. H., 48, 64
Brodigan, D. L., 18, 24, 30, 101, 102
Brotherson, M. J., 15, 155

Brown, J. E., 104, 107
Buncher, M. M., 48
Burton, J., 8
Buttram, J. L., 30
Byers, P. Y., 4, 7, 14, 18, 19, 152, 154

Calder, B. J., 8, 20, 24, 25, 26, 27, 49, 151
Cannon, A., 2
Chaubey, N. P., 63
Cochran, S. D., 24
Cohen, M. C., 30, 74, 92
Collins, C., 34
Connors, L., 31, 34
Cox, K. K., 8
Craig, J. R., 31
Crawford, P., 71

Dellens, M., 34
Dereshiwsky, M. I., 20
Diamond, S. G., 52
Dorgan, R. E., 61
Durgee, J., 25
Dyson, J. W., 63

Egbert, H. A., 103
Elbaum, B., 26
Elliott, D. B., 30
Elrod, J. M., 59, 69, 71
Engleberg, I. N., 30, 74, 92
Erkut, S., 7

Fedder, C. J., 66
Fern, E. F., 64
Fields, J. P., 7
Finnis, S., 34
Folch-Lyon, E., 5, 9, 19, 50, 64, 105
Frontczak, N. T., 103, 113
Fry, C. L., 62

Gall, J. P., 58
Gall, M. D., 58
Given, C. W., 34
Glaser, B. G., 104
Glesne, C., 98
Godwin, P. H. B., 63
Gold, R. S., 30
Goldman, A. E., 2
Goldstucker, J. L., 2
Goodman, R. I., 8, 27, 49
Gordon, J., 130
Gordon, W., 74, 89
Greenbaum, T. L., 9, 87, 89
Guba, E. G., 104, 114

Haager, D., 29, 77
Halasa, O., 34
Hammond, M., 28
Hamon, R. R., 34
Hanson, M., 31
Hazelwood, L. A., 63
Hess, J. M., 14
Higgenbotham, J. B., 8
Hillebrandt, I. S., 19, 20
Hisrich, R. D., 19, 24, 27
Huberman, A. M., 114, 115
Hughes, M. T., 16
Hyland, M. E., 34

Irvine, S. H., 34

Jallad, B., 33, 100
Johnson, D. K., 98
Johnston, K., 71

Karger, T., 20, 101
Kehoe, W. J., 25
Kelly, M. A., 30
Kendall, P. L., 4, 6
King, S., 34
Kitano, M. K., 112
Kleiner, R. E., 128
Klingner, J., 28
Kouzekanani, K., 130
Krueger, R. A., 2, 4, 9, 20, 30, 72, 102, 105

Langer, J., 84
Leavell, A. G., 31, 130
Lederman, L. C., 7, 17, 19, 64, 104
Lengua, L. J., 34, 62
Lewis, R. B., 112
Lincoln, Y. S., 104, 114
Lindgren, J. H., 25
Lynch, E. W., 112
Lyons, L., 49, 69

Marsigila, F. F., 34
Mates, D., 27
Maxwell, J., 98
Mays, V. M., 24
McCormick, W., 30
McDonald, S. S., 2
McDonald, W. J., 131, 138
McIntyre, S. H., 49, 146, 152, 154
McQuarrie, E. F., 49, 146, 152, 154
Mehrabian, A., 52
Merton, R. K., 3, 4, 6
Miles, M. B., 114, 115
Miller, W. J., 30
Moody, S., 26
Morgan, D. L., 2, 15, 18, 27, 96, 152
Murfin, P., 130

National Association for Independent Colleges and Universities, 81

Nelson, J. E., 103, 113
Niarhos, F. J., 130
Nolan, M. J., 34

Packard, F. D., 20
Patterson, L., 32
Patton, M. Q., 59, 98
Pauc, F., 29
Peshkin, A., 98
Peters, M. P., 19, 24, 27
Petersen, K. K., 34

Quiriconi, R. J., 61

Redfield, D. L., 31
Reitan, H. T., 63
Reynolds, F. D., 98
Ringo, S. A., 74
Rosenstein, A. J., 27
Ruhe, J. A., 63

Santa, C. M., 32
Sapolsky, A., 62
Saumell, L., 33, 130
Schoenfeld, G., 19
Schumm, J. S., 16, 26, 28, 29, 31, 33,
    34, 77, 100, 130
Schuster, C. S., 132
Shamdasani, P. N., 10, 53, 146
Share, S., 4
Shaw, M. E., 63

Short, K. G., 32
Slusher, J., 33
Smelser, W. T., 62
Smith, K. H., 32, 63
Spanish, M. T., 15, 18, 27, 152
Spethmann, B., 132, 133, 135
Stewart, D. W., 10, 53, 146
Stommel, M., 34
Strauss, A. L., 104
Strother, R. D., 17
Stycos, J. M., 2, 27

Thiessen, J. D., 34
Topper, G. E., 131, 138
Trombetta, W. L., 4
Trost, J. F., 5, 9, 19, 50, 64, 105

Vaughn, S., 16, 26, 28, 29, 31, 33, 34,
    77, 100, 130

Ward, V. M., 29, 104
Wells, W. D., 16, 50, 83, 144
Wilcox, J. R., 4, 7, 14, 18, 19, 152, 154
Wolf, K. P., 34

Yin, R. K., 60, 98, 113
Yoell, W. A., 50
Yuhas, P. L., 27, 28

Zeller, R. A., 18

Subject Index

Action research, 31-33
Adolescents:
  composition of groups, 132-133
  discussions with, 134-135
  establishing rapport with, 138
  opening remarks, 135-139
  parents and guardians, 139-140
  permission for participation, 139-141
  students in focus group interviews,
    130
Advertising, 2-3
Ages:
  minimum, for children, 132
  of participants, 63
AIDS education, use of focus group
    interviews, 24, 30
Applications of focus group interviews:
  action research, 31-33
  advertising, 2-3
  business, 7-8
  clinical research, 25
  communication research, 8, 14
  consumer satisfaction measurement,
    31
  exploratory research, 24-25
  health research and education, 8-9,
    24, 30

hypothesis development, 27
instrument development, 27-28
marketing, 2-3, 7-8
needs assessment, 30-31
phenomenological research, 25-26
policy development, 30
pretrial preparation, 31
program planning, 30
research design refinement, 28
research findings interpretation,
  28-29
Attendance:
  encouraging, 69-73
  no shows, 51

Beloit College, 30
Bias:
  during focus group interviews,
    152-153
  of moderators, 87-88, 89-90, 153
  socially desirable responses, 152
Body language, 84-85
  including in data analysis, 154
Brainstorming, 10
Business, use of focus group
    interviews, 7-8

Categorizing data, 107-109
    negotiating, 109-111
    See also Data analysis
Children:
    activities for, 138-139
    age limits, 132
    approaches to research with, 131
    composition of groups, 132-133
    developmental levels, 133
    discussions with, 134-135
    disruptive, 133
    ethical issues, 140-142
    informed consent, 141
    introductions, 139
    lengths of focus group interviews,
        132
    moderators for, 134-135
    need for comfortable atmosphere,
        138-139, 152
    opening remarks, 135-139
    parents and guardians, 139-140
    permission for participation, 139-141
    psychology research with, 130-131
    questions for, 134-135
    size of groups, 132
    students, 130
Clinical approach to research, 25
Clinicians, recruiting for focus group
        interviews, 66
Closing statements, 47-48
Communication research, 8, 14
Community colleges, use of focus
        group interviews, 30
Compatibility, of participants, 62
Computers, use in data analysis, 106,
        113-114, 115, 116-117
Confidentiality, 47, 69
Constant Comparative Method, 104
Consumer satisfaction, assessing with
        focus group interviews, 31
Costs, 148-149
    incentives, 72, 73

Data analysis:
    approaches, 103-104, 125
    categorizing data, 107-109
    computers used in, 106, 113-114,
        115, 116-117

concerns of researchers, 98
    considerations in, 111
    description of subjects, 99, 100
    identifying themes, 107-109, 112
    including nonverbal responses, 154
    margin coding, 107
    multiple focus groups, 111-112
    negotiating categories, 109-111
    pitfalls, 153-154
    preparation, 99-103
    procedure, 104-112
    rating quality of ideas, 113
    sorting information units, 108, 112
    summarizing key ideas after focus
        group interviews, 102-103
    theory as framework, 113
    transcript preparation, 101-102
    unitizing, 105-106
Delphi technique, 10

Education:
    questions addressed with focus
        group interviews, 26, 34
    students in focus groups, 130
    teacher-as-researcher movement, 32
    use of focus group interviews, 8, 15,
        33
Ethical issues:
    for outside moderators, 150
    in children's groups, 140-142
    in use of focus group interviews, 32
Ethnicity, 152
Experts, 63
    genuine, 83
    pseudo, 83
Exploratory approach to research, 24-25

Facilities:
    children's groups, 133-134, 140
    comfortable environment, 79-81
    distractions in, 52, 134
    furniture, 52, 53, 54, 133-134
    location of, 53-54
    recording equipment, 52, 80, 134
    room size, 52, 53
    seating arrangements, 52, 80,
        133-134

selecting, 51-52, 123-124
waiting room for parents, 140
Focused interviews. *See* Focus group
  interviews
Focus group interviews:
  advantages over individual
    interviews, 14, 19
  background, 2-4
  benefits, 2-3, 14, 16-20, 155
  checklist, 126
  costs, 148-149
  data quality, 98
  definitions, 4-5
  efficiency of, 20
  goals, 39-40, 121
  length of time, 50, 132
  misconceptions, 32
  multiple, 48-50, 60, 123
  observers, 77-78
  origins, 3-4
  pitfalls, 148-153
  popularity, 2
  potential misuses, 146-148
  preparation, 49
  process, 4
  purpose, 5-6, 38-39, 120
  types of data collected, 26
  underlying assumptions, 7, 17
  uses, 6-7, 40
  versatility, 15
  See also Applications of focus group
    interviews
Food, 71, 79
Furniture, 52, 53, 54
  for children's groups, 133-134

Gender, 62-63
  in groups of children and
    adolescents, 132
  mixed groups, 63
  same-sex groups, 63, 132
Generalizability, 60, 154-155
General purpose statements, 38, 120
Goals. *See* Objectives
Group depth interviews. *See* Focus
  group interviews
Group discussions, distinction from
  focus group interviews, 4, 5-6, 10

Guardians, 139-140

Health research and education, 8-9,
  24, 30
Heterogeneous groups, 62
Homogeneous groups, 58, 62
Hypothesis development and testing,
  27

Incentives, for participants, 72, 73
Individual interviews, 14, 19
Informed consent, 141
Instrument development, 27-28
Interview guides. *See* Moderator guides
Introductions, 41-42, 77-78
  in children's groups, 139

Lazarsfeld, Paul, 3

Margin coding, 107
Marketing research, focus group
  interviews, 2-3, 7-8
Member checks, 46-47, 101
Men. *See* Gender
Merton, R. K., 3
Minnesota Extension Service, 30
Minority groups. *See* Ethnicity
Moderator aides, 51, 93
Moderator guides, 41-48, 124
  children's groups, 134-135, 136-137
  clarification of terms, 43-44
  closing statements, 47-48
  importance of, 148
  introduction, 41-42
  level of detail, 41
  member checks, 46-47
  questions, 44-45
  sections, 43
  warm-up, 42-43
  wrap-up, 45-46
Moderators:
  biases, 87-88, 89-90, 153
  body language, 84-85
  characteristics, 85-87, 88, 149-150
  children's groups, 134-135

closing remarks, 85, 125
collecting useful data, 101
controlling topic, 81-85
creating comfortable environment,
    79-81, 151-152
cultural differences with
    participants, 152
ethical issues, 150
introductions, 41-42, 77-78, 139
leading discussion, 81-85, 86
need for flexibility, 18, 151
opening remarks, 42-43, 78-79, 80,
    124-125, 135-139
outside, 89, 90, 91-92, 150
personal interests, 88-90
pitfalls, 87-91, 149-150
planning, 76-77
posing questions, 81-82
preparation by, 76-77, 81, 124
qualifications, 89
selecting, 89, 120
setting up equipment, 80
taking notes, 101
training, 91-92, 149-150
welcoming participants, 77, 78
Motivations, of participants, 61, 69,
    71, 123

Naturalistic inquiry, 104
Nominal group technique, 10

Objectives, 39-40, 121
    information to obtain, 39-40
    See also Purpose statements
Observers:
    disclosing to participants, 77-78
    ethical considerations, 78
Outcomes, 40

Parents, 139-140
Participants:
    ages, 63, 132
    anonymity of responses, 47, 69
    behavioral types, 61
    candor of, 19

characteristics, 61-62
compatibility, 62
encouraging attendance, 69-73
experts, 63, 83
gender, 62-63, 132
heterogeneous groups, 62
homogeneous groups, 58, 62
incentives for, 72, 73
late arrivals, 51, 73
member checks, 46-47, 101
motivations, 61, 69, 71, 123
no shows, 51
number of, 50-51
opinions formed during focus group
    sessions, 20, 153
permission forms, 69, 70
personality types, 61
providing information to, 69,
    122-123
recruiting, 64-68, 150-151
reluctant, 151
screening procedure, 64, 122
selection criteria, 60-64, 121-122
socially desirable responses, 152
strangers, 63-64, 132-133
uninvolved, 84-85
value of direct contact with, 16-18
verbose, 84, 85
See also Adolescents; Children;
    Sampling
Permission:
    for children's participation, 139-141
    forms, 69, 70
    informed consent, 141
Personality types, of participants, 61
Philadelphia, Research for Better
    Schools Incorporated, 30
Policy development, use of focus group
    interviews, 29-31
Polling techniques, 84
Preparation:
    by moderators, 76-77, 81, 124
    for data analysis, 99-103
    for focus group interviews, 49
Pretrial preparation, 31
Prince George's Community College,
    92
Probes, 82

in children's groups, 135
Psychology:
  children and adolescents in focus
    groups, 130-131
  research questions, 34
  use of focus group interviews, 8, 15,
    33
Purpose statements:
  general, 38, 120
  refining, 38-39, 121
Purposive sampling, 58-60, 150

Qualitative research:
  compatibility of focus group
    interviews with, 15-16
  data types, 26
  goals, 155
  paradigm, 15-16
  sampling procedures, 58-60
  See also Data analysis
Quantitative data, 98
Questions, in focus group interviews:
  children's groups, 134-135
  closed, 82
  difficult, 45
  easy, 44-45, 81-82
  open-ended, 82
Questions, research, 26, 33-34
  for children and adolescents, 130
  inappropriate for focus groups,
    146-147
  in education, 26, 34
  in psychology, 34

Race. *See* Ethnicity
Recordings:
  equipment, 52, 80, 134
  reviewing, 102
  transcribing, 101-102
Recruiting participants, 64-68
  follow-up letters, 68
  guidelines for, 66-68
  problems with, 150-151
  referrals, 66
  target groups, 65
  through contact person, 65-66
  using membership lists, 65

Refreshments, 71, 79
Research:
  action, 31-33
  alternatives to focus group
    interviews, 10
  clinical approach, 25
  data collection, 26
  designs, 28
  exploratory approach, 24-25
  hypothesis development and testing,
    27
  instrument development, 27-28
  involving children, 130-131
  mistrust of, 151
  misuse of focus group interviews,
    146-147
  phenomenological approach, 25-26
  qualitative, 15-16, 58-60, 155
  questions appropriate for focus
    groups, 33-34
  questions for children and
    adolescents, 130
  use of focus group interviews, 6-7,
    14-15, 33
Research for Better Schools
  Incorporated, 30
Research teams:
  agreeing on purpose statements, 38,
    120
  moderators from, 89
Rooms. *See* Facilities

Sampling:
  boundaries, 60-61
  convenience, 59, 150-151
  pitfalls, 150
  plans, 58-60
  purposive, 58-60, 150
  random, 59
  types of, 59
Scheduling, 71
  children's groups, 139-140
Schools, recruiting participants
  through, 65, 66
Screening procedure, for participants,
  64, 122
Setting. *See* Facilities
Sex. *See* Gender

Software, for data analysis, 114, 115,
    116-117
Students. *See* Adolescents; Children
Subjects. *See* Participants
Synectics, 10

Teacher-as-researcher movement, 32
Teachers, recruiting for focus group
    interviews, 66
Themes, 107-109, 112
    See also Data analysis
Therapeutic approach to research, 25
Training, for moderators, 91-92
Transcripts:
    analyzing, 102
    level of detail, 102
    preparing, 101-102
    recording nonverbal responses, 154
    verifying, 102

    See also Data analysis

Unitizing data, 105-106
    categorizing, 107-109
    sorting, 108, 112
    See also Data analysis
Use of focus groups. *See* Applications
    of focus group interviews

Video. *See* Recordings

Warm-up, by moderator, 42-43
Women. *See* Gender
World War II, focus groups during, 3

Wrap-up, 45-46

ABOUT THE AUTHORS

Sharon Vaughn is a Professor in the Department of Teaching and Learning and the Department of Psychology at the University of Miami. Her primary research interests are social functioning of youngsters with learning disabilities and teachers' adaptations for students with learning disabilities. She received her Ph.D. from the University of Arizona.

Jeanne Shay Schumm is an Associate Professor in the Department of Teaching and Learning at the University of Miami. Her primary research interests include general education teachers' planning and adaptations for reading instruction for students with learning disabilities. She received her Ph.D. from the University of Miami.

Jane M. Sinagub, M.S.Ed., is a doctoral student in counseling psychology at the University of Miami. She serves as a research assistant in the School of Education Office of School-Based Research. Her interest is in human development and specifically the impact societal influences have on the maturation of females and males. Her research areas include methods for enhancing self-concept in school and obstacles to female participation in elementary and secondary classrooms.